SOURCES OF NEW TESTAMENT GREEK

SOURCES

OF

NEW TESTAMENT GREEK

OR

*THE INFLUENCE OF THE SEPTUAGINT
ON THE VOCABULARY OF THE
NEW TESTAMENT*

BY THE

REV. H. A. A. KENNEDY, M.A., D.Sc.

WIPF & STOCK · Eugene, Oregon

Wipf and Stock Publishers
199 W 8th Ave, Suite 3
Eugene, OR 97401

Sources of New Testament Greek
The Influence of the Septuagint on the Vocabulary of the New Testament
By Kennedy, H. A. A.
ISBN 13: 978-1-5326-1878-9
Publication date 3/10/2017
Previously published by T. & T. Ckark, 1895

PREFACE

In the preface to his *Essays in Biblical Greek*, the late Dr. Hatch speaks of these as being designed "to point out to students of sacred literature some of the rich fields which have not yet been adequately explored, and to offer suggestions for their exploration." This book is an attempt to deal with some of the matters which formed the subject of Dr. Hatch's investigation, and, indeed, owes its origin to the results at which that most independent and keen-minded scholar arrived as regards the special character of Biblical Greek. But while the writer began with a complete, though provisional, acceptance of Hatch's conclusions, the farther the inquiry was pushed, the more decidedly was he compelled to doubt those conclusions, and finally to seek to establish the connection between the language of the LXX. and that of the New Testament on a totally different basis.

The discussion is purely a tentative one. Further research may modify many of the results which are here presented. But it seems to the writer that the lines for investigation laid down in this dissertation are at least trustworthy, and lead to the true standpoint for the study of Biblical Greek as a whole.

A list of the chief authorities referred to and consulted is given. But the writer must express special obligations to two books—Mullach's *Grammatik der griechischen Vulgarsprache*, and Thayer's edition of Grimm's *Lexicon of the New Testament*. The admirable lists in the Appendix to the latter work have formed, to a large extent, the basis of this investigation.

CALLANDER,
February 1895.

CONTENTS

CHAPTER I

INTRODUCTION . . . 1

CHAPTER II

NATURE AND SCOPE OF THE SUBJECT

Limitations of such an inquiry — Its possibilities — Method of investigation 5–10

CHAPTER III

CONDITIONS AND CIRCUMSTANCES OF THE GREEK LANGUAGE IN THE THIRD CENTURY B.C.

The Attic of Xenophon and its formative elements—The new spirit—The Macedonian dialect—Transition-stage of language in Aristotle—Character of the Attic diffused by Alexander's conquests—The literary dialect 11–20

CHAPTER IV

THE SEPTUAGINT: (1) ITS ENVIRONMENT; (2) ITS VOCABULARY, AND THE SPECIAL INFLUENCES WHICH MOULD IT

General character of Egyptian Greek—The language of Alexandria—Origin of the Septuagint—Special considerations affecting the investigation of the vocabulary of the Septuagint—Tables illustrating the various elements in the vocabulary: (1) old poetical words; (2) Ionic words; (3) affinities with Xenophon and the writers of the κοινή; (4) colloquial words; (5) diminutives in common with the Comic writers; (6) new formations; (6) foreign words 21–45

viii   CONTENTS

CHAPTER V

PAGE

BRIEF SURVEY OF THE MAIN FACTS IN THE HISTORY OF THE VOCABULARY OF GREEK LITERATURE FROM ABOUT (200-160 B.C.) THE COMPLETION OF THE SEPTUAGINT DOWN TO *c*. 100 A.D.

The "Common" and "Hellenistic" dialects as parallel growths — The Common dialect — Polybius — The writers of the Apocrypha—Philo—Josephus—Plutarch—Summary of results 46–59

CHAPTER VI

THE VOCABULARY OF THE NEW TESTAMENT

Problems affecting the investigation of the vocabulary—Numerical statistics—General tone of the language—Tables illustrating the elements in the vocabulary — The classical element — Affinities with the writers of the κοινή — The colloquial element: Points of contact with Comic writers; lists; affinities with Aristophanes—Parallels between the Greek of the Comic Fragments and the late language—Colloquial element, continued : Weakening of strong terms   .   . 60–83

CHAPTER VII

COMPARISON OF THE VOCABULARY OF THE LXX. WITH THAT OF THE NEW TESTAMENT

The LXX. familiar to the New Testament writers—Dr. Hatch's dicta—Classification of possible relations between two vocabularies—List of words peculiar to LXX. and New Testament— List of words peculiar to LXX. and New Testament along with Philo—List of words common to LXX. and New Testament with "Biblical" meaning—Summary of results   . 84–93

CHAPTER VIII

THE INFLUENCE OF THE LXX. ON THE THEOLOGICAL AND RELIGIOUS TERMS OF THE NEW TESTAMENT VOCABULARY

Formation of a theological terminology — Discussion of words exemplifying the influence of the LXX. on the theological and religious terms of the New Testament—Cautions to be observed in estimating this influence .   .   .   94–109

CONTENTS ix

CHAPTER IX

DISCUSSION OF VARIOUS CLASSES OF WORDS IN THE NEW TESTAMENT, WHICH EITHER IN THEMSELVES OR BY THEIR PARTICULAR USES SUGGEST A CONNECTION WITH THE LXX.

Actual Hebrew words — Words expressing Jewish customs and ideas—Words with exceptional meanings in the LXX. and New Testament — "Alexandrian" words—New compound words 110–133

CHAPTER X

DISCUSSION OF THE GENERAL QUESTION OF THE INFLUENCE OF THE LXX. ON THE VOCABULARY OF THE NEW TESTAMENT, BASED ON THE RESULTS REACHED

Subdivision of the New Testament vocabulary — Numerical statistics—Exaggeration of the influence of the LXX. on the vocabulary of the New Testament — Marked differences between the two vocabularies—Application of the criteria laid down on p. 87 sq., to the case of the LXX. and New Testament 134–145

CHAPTER XI

COLLOQUIAL GREEK, THE LANGUAGE OF THE LXX. AND OF THE NEW TESTAMENT

The striking resemblances between the language of the two groups of writings due to its "colloquial" character in both —Statistics — The spoken language, and its diffusion and developments—Distinction between the colloquialism of the New Testament and that of the LXX. . . . 146–151

CHAPTER XII

CORROBORATION OF THE COLLOQUIAL CHARACTER OF THE LANGUAGE OF THE LXX. AND NEW TESTAMENT BY THE PHENOMENA OF MODERN GREEK

Introductory note on the continuity of the spoken language down to modern times — Brief discussions of illustrative examples 152–156

CHAPTER XIII

EXAMINATION OF PECULIAR FORMS WHICH GO TO PROVE THE COLLOQUIAL CHARACTER OF THE LANGUAGE OF THE LXX. AND NEW TESTAMENT

	PAGE
Prefatory Remarks—Verb-forms—"Popular" spellings .	157–164
SUMMARY OF RESULTS	164–166
LIST OF AUTHORITIES	167
INDEX OF GREEK WORDS	171

SOURCES OF NEW TESTAMENT GREEK

CHAPTER I

INTRODUCTION

THE study of Language, like all other provinces of investigation, has been influenced to a high degree by the modern scientific spirit. Not that this influence has come from without and forced itself upon philological inquiry. The process has been evolved from within, and under conditions marked for it by the principles inherent in Language itself. One main result is that the sphere of investigation is ever being widened. Light is thrown on important problems from directions the most various. Fine Art, Antiquities strictly so called, Epigraphy, Folk-lore, each contributes its quota to linguistic research.

But perhaps nothing has tended so powerfully to give this particular department a place among the exact sciences as the rapid advance which the latter half of the present century has seen in the field of Comparative Philology. Now, investigations in this province have not only reached results quite invaluable in themselves, and for their own sake, but have brought into prominence certain leading conceptions in regard to language in general which will inevitably impress themselves on all future study.

Not the least important is that which regards a particular language as a living whole, an organic unity, which, while from time to time it presents varying aspects, retains an indestructible common principle which is really a thread of life, preserving it throughout its entire history from utter disintegration. In this way, every stage of a language is of paramount importance for the history of the whole. Of course, some periods will always have, and justly have, a special attraction. The reasons are various. One stage of a language becomes of special moment because it is the formative epoch. It displays the birth, so to speak, of the principles which are to be the determining elements throughout the history of the speech. Another stage absorbs interest as the culminating point, the zenith in the language's life. All rudimentary strivings after expression have been mastered. The language has become plastic. It is an artistic instrument. Its products are works of art. It has a freeness and largeness of sweep, it has a grasp of technical details. There is balance, symmetry, proportion. No doubt this will correspond to a unique era in the nation's history. The life of the people is untramelled and broad. The national spirit has reached a summit, and this wealth of splendid energy calls for expression. It creates expression. So the language becomes the mirror of the national life. It is therefore necessary that this definite period should, above all others, call for consideration. And in any language, but especially in one so rich, and subtle, and strong as that of Hellas, a grasp of its culminating epoch and its great masters is that which alone affords a standpoint from which to survey the language as a whole. When that epoch closes, the Greek tongue enters on a new and, in many aspects, disastrous career.

But, though its grace and charm are seriously impaired, though corruption spreads with extraordinary rapidity, the history of the language never loses in interest. Indeed, the interest deepens as we find it striving to become the world-speech, passing through a new mould of foreign influences and alien tongues, and coming forth with the stamp of cosmopolitanism upon it, the fitting instrument of a world-wide empire.

The later stages, therefore, of Greek have a special importance of their own. On the one hand, they are a comment on the earlier life of the language, inasmuch as they show the forces inherent in that life, their powers of self-preservation, the points where they are liable to attack, the conditions determining their development or decay. On the other hand, they look forward to the future, revealing the particular adaptabilities of the Hellenic tongue, suggesting its lines of further dissemination, affording in a special case a remarkable forecast of modern linguistic developments. But not this alone. The corruption has in it seeds of life. In this decaying stage of Greek, striking light is shed on many phenomena which otherwise would appear abnormal in the history of the language. Its latent resources are displayed with a new and astonishing clearness. So that, on the whole, the materials gained by investigation of Greek when its palmy days were over, are both valuable in themselves, and exceptionally valuable for the insight they give into the innate essence, and potencies, and influence of the speech of the Hellenic peoples, viewed in its entirety.

CHAPTER II

NATURE AND SCOPE OF THE SUBJECT

ONE of these later stages of the Greek language has been taken as the subject of this Dissertation. Or rather the attempt is made to trace some special elements in the history of Greek through several stages. But in endeavouring to estimate " The Influence of the Septuagint on the Vocabulary of the New Testament," it is necessary to make a preliminary inquiry as to the general nature and scope of an investigation like this, its limitations and its possibilities, the results which may be expected and those which need not be.

An investigation like the present must be entirely tentative, for the important reason that the language of the Septuagint, as a whole, has never been accurately or rigidly examined and classified. Indeed, anything like precise assertion must be made from the New Testament as starting-point. Much has been written in a vague way as to points of contact between the two groups of writings, but when one attempts to distinguish some solid facts which may be taken as results arrived at, scarcely any such are to be found among a hazy mass of broad asseverations. This holds as to the relations of the language of the Septuagint to that of the New

Testament, viewed generally. But, no doubt, definiteness is not so easily reached in such inquiries. Especially is such a statement true of our subject which deals with the language of these two large collections of books, in one particular aspect, the relation of their *vocabularies*. Yet this means a definitely-marked province, a fact which, to some extent at least, may preserve our investigation from mere vague generalities.

One fixed point there is from which to start, and that is the vocabulary of the New Testament, which is being investigated from year to year with increasing accuracy and scientific precision. Working back from this to the Septuagint, we gain lines of procedure and standpoints for a general survey. The object of our inquiry is to ascertain, as far as possible, the various stages in the development of the so-called "Hellenistic" dialect of Greek, its relations to the literary language of contemporary writers, and the amount of its connection with the colloquial language of the period. For this purpose a distinct field of investigation is necessary, and that chosen appears, in some points at least, adequate to the end aimed at.

The limitations of the subject are not hard to discover. It need scarcely be said that it would be impossible within reasonable limits to take up the separate vocabularies of the various writers either of the New Testament or Septuagint. In the case of the latter, absolutely so, as the various hands in its compilation can only be hypothetically distinguished. But this is not necessary. In any case only approximate results could be looked for, and so, roughly speaking, our inquiry is in no way hampered by taking each group of writings as a whole. In the case of the New Testament, of course, a period of about fifty years comprises all the writers. Perhaps a hundred and fifty would be nearer the mark as regards the Septuagint; but the Pentateuch, which all scholars admit to be the nucleus of the whole translation, and its most careful part, may be regarded in all probability as finished within less than half that time.

But there is a further limitation inseparable from the subject. The comparison of two vocabularies must always be a relative process. In this inquiry it is especially so. For not only is each of these vocabularies made up of several types of language, so to speak, due to writers of varying individuality, but we possess no contemporary literature of precisely the same class which might be used as a standard or norm to guide our determinations. Accordingly we must often be content with provisional results, the only ones which can be arrived at with our present data.

Still further, the estimation of the influence of one vocabulary upon another has a certain incalculable element which must not be lost sight of. The biography of words is often almost incredible. Thus, a word peculiar in form and of uncouth appearance may be found in the Septuagint repeatedly as the translation of a more or less common idea. This word may occur nowhere else save in the New Testament. But constantly it has a submerged history. It may be a local peculiarity. It may be a derivation from some special dialect, all the circumstances of which are unknown. It may be one of the most common forms of the vernacular.

It may have become stereotyped by means of the Septuagint, and thus have passed into the New Testament through its direct influence. All these possibilities and more will present themselves, and often it will be impossible to come to a decision. Again, in the two vocabularies with which we are concerned, there is, of course, an unusual number of terms which express moral and religious and theological conceptions. But it is quite possible that an unusual term which is found in the one may be found in the other with something like a complete change of content. No doubt this can be usually determined with a sufficient degree of accuracy. Still, as regards the influence of the one vocabulary on the other, in such cases the question is a delicate one, in which hasty assertions are unsafe. Once more, the conditions under which each of the vocabularies is found must not be overlooked as determining factors. It is here we are most heavily handicapped. It is not overstating the matter to say that our knowledge of the special circumstances which may have led the separate writers of the New Testament to display particular characteristics in their vocabularies is scanty in the extreme. More so is this true of the Greek translators of the Old Testament.

But in spite of all these limitations which look so formidable, there is a wide area for research, and results may be obtained more valuable than would have been anticipated. It does not affect the inquiry whether these are predominantly positive or predominantly negative. In either case, light will be thrown on biblical Greek as a whole.

But there are further important possibilities. The special phase of the Greek language which we have to consider has, at least, the advantage of being unartificial. So that we should expect side-lights on questions outside the scope of our main inquiry. Also, the subject brings us face to face with a peculiar phenomenon in the history of the Hellenic tongue; its employment by an alien and deeply-prejudiced race to set forth their own highest conceptions. This means a new demand on the resources of the Greek speech, a new test of its plasticity and scope. But besides, we have in the vocabularies of the Septuagint and New Testament, apart from special Hebraistic traits, a character and colouring quite distinct from the literary language of the time. Such a fact must suggest new points of view from which to regard the development of Greek in its later stages.

The most important feature has still to be emphasised. We have the right to expect that a very direct relation will be found to exist between the language of the Septuagint and that of the New Testament. There are various reasons for the expectation. The chief one is that these two groups of writing are the only monuments of the "dialect" they represent. This "dialect" attains definite form in the Septuagint. It has a fixed stamp put upon it. It is therefore natural to believe that when we meet it again it will show the impress of its earlier life. More especially will this be the case with conceptions and modes of thought peculiar to the Jewish people. The very fact that Greek is not their native language will be found to make it harder for them to deviate from a standard once laid down, especially when their own rites and usages and characteristics are involved. Reference has been already made to the abundance of terms which translate particular religions and theological ideas. With regard to them, we are justified in expecting that in many cases, at least, the language of the Septuagint will be found to be the basis on which the New Testament structure is reared.

Having examined the nature and scope of the investigation, we need not linger long over the method to be employed. Clearly the question is one of *facts*, and where there is so much room for hypothesis, its use must be scanty. Our first task is to ascertain as distinctly as possible the actual data which we possess. This is, indeed, the most important part of the inquiry. For here there is a solid foundation. But these data have to be viewed, above all, in their historical setting. If they can be connected by links of historical evidence, all will have been gained that can be gained. But whether or no, the investigation is a record of facts, and the inferences which these facts permit. It is useless to attempt anything more.

CHAPTER III

CONDITIONS AND CIRCUMSTANCES OF THE GREEK LANGUAGE IN THE THIRD CENTURY B.C.

THE first matter to be examined is necessarily the conditions and circumstances of the Greek language in the third century B.C., the period in which our inquiry starts. The tone and character of the Greek which then prevailed should give the key to its subsequent development. But it would be wrong to limit ourselves to this single epoch. It cannot be understood apart from currents and movements in the language which go back at least a century earlier, and which are anticipations of the processes which were afterwards to be dominant.

Nothing is more striking than the change which meets one on passing from the Attic of Plato and Demosthenes to that of Xenophon. At first sight the difference is not so obvious. But when we begin to examine rigorously the vocabulary of the earlier writer, it is easy to trace in him a totally divergent conception of what the range of Attic Greek is, and a complete disregard of its precise limitations. In making this statement, however, regard must be had to the well-known phenomenon, apparently peculiar to Attic, in which the earlier stage of the dialect, after becoming the parent of a new and more perfect form of speech, continued to exist in healthy vigour, and to be used exclusively for one particular type of poetical composition. This, of course, holds good of Athens alone. But this earlier Attic had countless affinities with the cognate Ionic speech prevailing in numerous regions of the Greek-speaking world. Indeed, that and the earliest Attic might be said to have the same basis.

It is difficult to conjecture even as to the relation between the earlier Attic, which always remained the vehicle of tragedy, and the popular spoken language of Athens in its best days, though probably there can be little doubt that the latter closely approximated in *kind*, if not always in *quality*, to the Greek of the orators and Aristophanes. But, at anyrate, this earlier Attic was known and recognised within certain limits, and it would be the delicate and subtle feeling for language which would chiefly secure the mature Attic against its encroachments.

To return to Xenophon. His experience was a peculiar one. His life was deliberately spent away from his native land, and a large portion of it in foreign countries outside Greece proper altogether. In this way he mingled with men of many dialects. His pride in Athens and her glory of life and language vanished. This must consciously or unconsciously affect his language also. His sense of proportion, his appreciation of the just mean to be observed, and the strict standard of speech, must unconsciously be marred. And so, in the midst of dialects cognate to his own, in which the subtle shades of meaning and the refinements of pure Attic were replaced by laxness of usage and clumsier notions of the requirements of language, he abandoned the purity of Athens and became a noteworthy precursor of the future history of the Greek tongue.

It is interesting to find the Mysian Galen, in his *Commentary on Hippocrates* (quoted by Rutherford, *New Phryn.* 161), comparing Xenophon with the celebrated physician in the use of ὀνόματα γλωσσηματικὰ καὶ τροπικά. And Helladius (fifth century A.D.) is quoted by Photius (*Bibl.* 533. 25) as saying: οὐδὲν θαυμαστὸν ἀνὴρ ἐν στρατείαις σχολάζων καὶ ξένων συνουσίαις εἴ τινα παρακόπτει τῆς πατρίου φωνῆς· διὸ νομοθέτην αὐτὸν οὐκ ἄν τις ἀττικισμοῦ παραλάβοι.

Many instances might be given to illustrate what has been said of Xenophon. The following (from Rutherford's list, *New Phryn.* 165 sq.) will suffice:—

ἀγρεύω, "hunt" = θηρεύω, κυνηγετῶ. Hipp. 4. 18; Cyn. 12. 6; *Anab.* 5. 3. 8; LXX., N.T.

ἁλίζω = ἀθροίζω. Cyr. 1. 4. 14; *Anab.* 7. 3. 48; Herod. 1. 79, 5. 15, 7. 12; Eurip. *Heracl.* 403; N.T.

δώρημα = δῶρον. *Hier.* 8. 4; Aesch. *P. V.* 626; *Pers.* 523; Soph. *Aj.* 662; Eurip. *Hel.* 883; N.T.

θάλπω = θερμαίνω. Cyr. 5. 1. 11; Hom. *Od.* 21. 179; Hes. *Theog.* 864; Aesch. *P. V.* 590; LXX., N.T.

θιγγάνω = ἅπτομαι. Cyr. 1. 3. 5, etc.; Aesch. *P. V.* 849, etc.; Soph. *Oed. R.* 760, etc.; Eur. *Hec.* 605, etc.; N.T. θίγω in LXX.

μόχθος = πόνος. *Conviv.* 2. 4, 8. 40; Hes. *Sc.* 306; Aesch., Soph., Eur., LXX., N.T.

νοσφίζω = ὑφαίρω. Cyr. 4. 2. 42; Aesch. *Cho.* 620; Soph. *Phil.* 1427; Eur. *Sup.* 153; LXX., N.T.

τάραχος = ταραχή. *Anab.* 1. 8. 2; Cyr. 7. 1. 32; Hippoc. 300. 41; LXX., N.T.

Already in Xenophon's days tokens of change in the fortunes of the Greek peoples might readily be found. Yet the separate States had sufficient pride of independence to preserve their national life a stage further. But the old restrictions of nationality could not much longer endure. A new spirit was beginning to pervade Greek life,—no doubt, in many aspects, a weaker and more nerveless spirit, yet one which contained within itself the potency of a wider civilisation, a more cosmopolitan existence. Thus it was that neighbouring peoples began to aspire to a new and higher cultivation. Barbarian Macedonia claimed a share in the refinements of her more polished neighbours. It need not be doubted that political motives had a large part in such aims. But, granting this, the issue was not affected. The Attic language became the language of the Macedonian Court. The modifications which it underwent in this new phase of its history cannot be accurately determined. For this purpose a clear notion would have to be formed of the precise character of the pre-existing Macedonian dialect. As it is, fragmentary hints must suffice as to its nature and constitution.

A passage in Curtius, vi. 9, § 35–36 (quoted by Mullach, *Grammatik*, p. 14), seems to say that Macedonians and Greeks could not understand one another. And certainly, if reliance can be placed on the collections made by Sturz (*De Dialecto Macedonica*, etc. pp. 30, 31 sq.) and others, it is no wonder that this was so. A few instances will make this clear.

    ἀκόντιον—among Macedonians = ῥάχις, chine, ridge. So Hesych. and Phavorinus.

δάνος = θάνατος (Plut. de aud. poet. 5).
κάραβος = πύλη. Hesych. Phavor.
ἀγκαλίς = δρέπανον.

Two of the words quoted in this connection have a more interesting history, viz. παρεμβολή and ῥυμή.

παρεμβολή, which seems properly to mean "insertion," "interpolation" is described by Phrynichus, 353, as δεινῶς Μακεδονικόν; and all the old grammarians apparently assent to this. Starting from its original signification, it would first come to mean "method of arrangement of camp," and finally reach its ordinary Macedonian sense of "camp," "encampment." It occurs often in Polybius = (1) Locatio in castris. Ipsa castra. (2) Aciei instructio. (3) Special manœuvres in a naval battle. It is found in an inscription of Thessalonica (c. 118 B.C.—Dittenberger, Syll.[1] 247. 20), μετεπέμψατο εἰς τὴν· παρεμβολήν. Countless instances in the Septuagint where, almost without exception, it translates the Hebrew term for "camp," "encampment." It occurs ten times in the New Testament. (1) Camp, Heb. 13. 11; Apoc. 20. 9. (2) Encampment, almost = army, Heb. 11. 34. (3) Barracks, Acts 21. 34, 22. 24, 23. 10. It is used in jest by Diphilus as = στρατόπεδον, and also found in the comic writers Theophilus (Mein. 3. 630), and Crito (Mein. 4. 53).

ῥύμη. Phryn. 382: ῥύμῃ· καὶ τοῦτο οἱ μὲν Ἀθηναῖοι ἐπὶ τῆς ὁρμῆς ἐτίθεσαν, οἱ δὲ νῦν ἀμαθεῖς ἐπὶ τοῦ στενώπου. δοκεῖ δέ μοι καὶ τοῦτο μακεδονικὸν εἶναι. Suidas explains ἀγυιαί by ῥύμῃ. Eustathius on Hom. Il. β. p. 166 (quoted by Sturz), says ῥύμη is used

[1] Sylloge Inscriptionum Græcarum, W. Dittenberger.

in this sense in the κοινή. The earlier signification of "*rush*," "onset," is found in places like Thucyd. 7. 70: τῇ μὲν πρώτῃ ῥύμῃ ἐπιπλέοντες κ.τ.λ.

Polyb. 6. 29. 1 : αἱ ῥύμαι = roads in a camp.

In the Septuagint: Isa. 15. 3 : καὶ ἐν ταῖς ῥύμαις αὐτῶν πάντες ὀλολύζετε = street. In the New Testament four times, and = street or lane. Used by the comic writers Antiphanes and Philippides = street (Mein. 3. 26, 4. 471). The stages in the history of the word are well pointed out by Carr (on Matt. vi. 2): (1) rush, impetus; (2) going; (3) lane or street; cf. English "alley," from French "aller."

We have dwelt longer on these two terms for a special reason. They open the way to a large question, the intermingling of foreign elements, or, at least, usages with the pure Greek tongue at an exceedingly early date. The constant voice of tradition makes them Macedonian words. But when we find them in Attic writers like Antiphanes (380 B.C.), Theophilus (330 B.C.), Crito (330 B.C. ?), Philippides (323 B.C.), and Diphilus (300 B.C.), the suggestion naturally presents itself that there was a far closer connection between the colloquial language of everyday life and the alien dialects of Greek than has usually been believed, or that original elements of current Attic speech were preserved outside the strict limits of the dialect. It would be absurd to make the slender basis of a few examples support any far-reaching hypothesis, but these give rise to the belief that if a greater mass of materials came to light, the problem would be far on its way towards solution.

But besides the appearance in the Macedonian dialect

of peculiar terms, such as ἀδῆ = οὐρανός, βέθυ = ἀήρ, δώραξ = σπλήν, and the like, peculiar consonantal changes are said to have prevailed, which appear to have a phonetic character; *e.g.* βαλακρός = φαλακρός, κεβαλή = κεφαλή, ἀδραία = αἰθρία κ.τ.λ. Probably such lists have to be taken with caution, as so little is known of the sources used by the old lexicographers who are our authorities. In any case, the Macedonian type of Greek, whether or not it is admissible to call it a special *dialect*, was so far removed from ordinary Attic as to make it certain that the latter, on Macedonian lips, must soon and inevitably suffer thoroughgoing modification. Even the Greek polish itself of Alexander the Great and his associates was only skin-deep.

But apart from the process of change experienced by the Attic dialect in a semi-barbarian country like Macedonia, the world of culture, as well, was opening the way for results of that kind. Aristotle himself marks the beginning of a new era. Looking at his language alone, one is struck by the number of new words and new forms which he admits into his prose. The perfect Attic sense for language seems to have become relaxed in him. The transition to the κοινή has already begun. Naturally, the tendency increases rapidly. It is found in an intensified degree in writers like Theophrastus, who may almost be reckoned with the writers of the "Common Dialect." And, as has often been pointed out, it is noteworthy that contemporaneous with this weakening of purity in language is the growth of the Asian rhetoric, which seeks to make up for nerve and force by florid colouring and exaggeration.

Thus, within Greece itself, the degeneration had set in.

Alexander's conquests formed the determining factor for the language, as for the whole life of the Greek peoples. Now, as has been said, the Attic dialect was undoubtedly recognised as the basis of the language spoken at the Macedonian court. This meant that henceforth the official and imperial speech throughout the Eastern world must be Attic at root, whatever varying aspects it might present in particular cases. It did not à priori follow that the language of the conquerors should become that of the conquered. But Greek civilisation had been making rapid advances. Even the interior had not been left wholly untouched. The maritime regions were already thoroughly leavened by Greek influence. But the language which Alexander and his victorious armies brought with them found special points of contact in the several countries through the remnants of old Greek colonies, so that, even in districts where they did not themselves settle as rulers, Greek idioms became familiar. The dialect which they introduced was Attic, but the Attic of a non-Athenian people. Accordingly, from the first, there would be a laxity as regards the words to be used, and the nature of their usage. This was an element sure to lead to further corruption. And so we find that in each province the Greek spoken there assumed a distinctly local colouring, reflecting at many points the dialect originally peculiar to that province. Our data on this point are somewhat fragmentary. But there are constant traces of local dialectical variations. We shall find the most noteworthy instances when we come to examine more carefully the Greek of Alexandria. But such phenomena as the late Aorist form in -οσαν, on which Eustathius, p. 1759, 36, says: οἱ τῇ Ἀσιανῇ χρώμενοι φωνῇ ποιοῦσι τὸ ἔφυγον καὶ ἦλθον παρενθέσει τῆς σα συλλαβῆς ἐφύγοσαν λέγοντες καὶ ἤλθοσαν. φωνῆς Χαλκιδέων ἴδια εἰσι; the substitution of the weak Aorist endings in strong forms, as ἔλαβα, ἔπεσα κ.τ.λ., which the old grammarians hold to be originally a Cilician peculiarity; and the appearance of many uncouth words in the later language, principally associated with the requirements of common life,—give some colour to the idea of a widespread local effect on the language which Alexander established in his new domain.

Another point has to be strongly emphasised. The one aim of the Macedonians who diffused the Attic type of Greek was to be intelligible. They had no thought for refinement of idiom or purity of vocabulary. They were not themselves cultivated men, and their language was not a cultivated language. The important consequence followed that it never became a literary instrument. No doubt this would have given it fixity and a standard. Instead, it became the parent of a new type of colloquial Greek, the speech of the mixed populations of Asia, Syria, and Egypt. This is a most important fact. All those who afterwards laid any claim to *literary* power or skill must be held rather to carry on the tradition of Aristotle and his contemporaries, than to belong immediately to the circle of the Ἑλληνίζοντες. Of course they are conditioned by their environment. The Greek which Aristotle had handed down to them was already in process of fusion. Words, forms, and phrases distinctly non-Attic had been admitted by him. It would be absurd to suppose that amidst the mixed populations of the countries where these writers lived, the tendency already manifested could be checked. Everything was in favour of its growth. Still, it was regulated and kept, to some extent, within bounds by the general culture of these writers, their acquaintance with the early literature of Greece, and a more or less earnest attempt to preserve alive the literary succession by direct imitation of some of the great masters of speech.

Thus arose the literary language, the κοινὴ διάλεκτος. More will have to be said of it in tracing the linguistic history between the time of the Septuagint and that of the New Testament. No doubt great caution must be used in drawing a strict dividing-line between the literary dialect and the colloquial speech of everyday life. We must rather regard the boundary as fluctuating and undefined. Yet it may be said that while the writers of the κοινή frequently descend to the ordinary level of the current popular language, or nearly so, the literary monuments which we have of that popular language rarely reach, so far as style and idiom and even purity of vocabulary are concerned, the common standard of the κοινὴ διάλεκτος.

CHAPTER IV

THE SEPTUAGINT: (1) ITS ENVIRONMENT; (2) ITS VOCABULARY, AND THE SPECIAL INFLUENCES WHICH MOULD IT

AFTER the foregoing very brief account of the general condition of language in which the LXX. arose, we must next investigate its immediate environment, and this will form the transition to the discussion of our special subject itself.

In no country did Macedonian influence produce more rapid and far-reaching effects than in Egypt. Alexandria, the capital, founded under the auspices of the Macedonian conqueror, formed a centre of new prosperity for the country. Favoured by natural situation, the glory of its founding, and the benign rule of the early Ptolemies, it could not fail to be a most potent instrument in the diffusion of Hellenism among the Eastern peoples. As has been already said, the Macedonians brought with them, as their ordinary language, the Attic dialect, not, however, unadulterated and pure, but modified in many directions by reason of having become their official and conventional mode of speech. Accordingly, Egypt too must yield to the new tongue. Not, of course, that Greek was a strange language there, but that from this time it was to be *the* language of court life and letters, of trade and commerce, soon also, through the mixed population of a great national centre like Alexandria, the language of common life and ordinary intercourse. Now the conditions under which the Macedonian Attic took root in Egypt could only lead to *one* result. Nowhere was there a more remarkable blending of diverging elements than at Alexandria. Egyptians, pure Greeks, Macedonians, representatives of the various Asiatic kingdoms, Africans, Jews, all combined to form a motley crowd; yet they must have constant dealings with one another. The medium of intercourse must inevitably be Greek. It was impossible that it could retain even the purity of its Macedonian type among elements so conflicting.

The question accordingly arises, What special colour would Greek, as spoken by the Egyptian people, be likely to assume? We know that they had deep-seated Oriental tendencies. We are told that their temperament was melancholy; that they were possessed by a strong bias towards the formless symbolism of their ancient worship; that their imagination was eager and excitable. Accordingly, we are not surprised to find from the remains preserved, a certain unwieldiness and capriciousness about their language, which displays itself especially in harsh and fantastic word-composition. Besides, this might naturally be looked for, as Greek came to them, not by free and spontaneous diffusion, but in the stilted guise of officialism.

Many instances from their vocabulary, as exhibited by the Rosetta Inscription, Papyri, etc. etc., are given by

Mullach, Bernhardy, and others. From these the following are taken:—

ἀδίκιον, αἰωνόβιος, ἀποδιεσταλμένων, αὐτοκρασίᾳ, ἐπάναγκον, ζημιοπρακτήσειν, ἱερισσῶν, κατανωτιζόμενος, κουφοτελειῶν, λογένειν, οὐσιακός, παρασυγγράφειν, πρωτοπραξίᾳ, τὸ τελεστικόν, φιλανθρωπεῖν.

As to the Greek of Alexandria proper, it seems erroneous to give it the name of a dialect, as many scholars have been accustomed to do. In all probability the language of the Egyptian capital had no more right to be called a dialect than the vernacular of any other great centre of population and commerce. On the other hand, it does appear that, owing to the unique position and circumstances of Alexandria, a certain type of Greek arose there, or was stereotyped there, which was rapidly diffused. It was no literary language, and could not be. It was a blending of words and idioms on an Attic basis, contributed to the common stock by the shifting masses which made up the population of the city. Thus East and West alike impressed their stamp on the Alexandrian speech.

There is no need to say, as some scholars have asserted, that no memorial of the Alexandrian type of Greek has come down to us. We believe that the more the language of the LXX. is studied, the more clearly it will be seen that, in spite of strong Hebrew colouring and the moulding force of Jewish conceptions, the LXX. does afford a lucid and graphic view of the Greek of Alexandria. And more importance attaches itself to this because Alexandrian Greek may be regarded as a typical representative of the language then spoken throughout the provinces which had yielded to Alexander's sway.

It is unnecessary for us here to do more than state the views generally held by modern scholars regarding the date and origin of the Greek translation of the Old Testament. There is a consensus of opinion that the whole, or, in any case, the greater part of the undertaking, was carried out at Alexandria. This rests on an unbroken line of tradition. The question cannot be decided as to whether any of the kings took a special interest in the work. A mass of legend has grown round this report. The nucleus of the translation was the Pentateuch, a fact to be expected, seeing that for the Jews the reading of the Law formed the chief part of synagogue worship. In all probability this portion of the Old Testament was translated about the middle of the third century B.C., and the prologue to "Ecclesiasticus" says that by 130 B.C., not only the "Law" but the "Prophets" and the other books of the Old Testament were extant in Greek. The translation, as a whole, reveals several hands, at least five, differing to a considerable degree in acquaintance with Greek, power of grasping the original, and skill in translating. The Pentateuch has been done by the most competent translators. The internal character of the version makes it almost certain that the translators were *Egyptian* Jews. Thus, to give one or two instances—

(1)[1] The Hebrew "shekel" is translated by the Alexandrian "didrachmum," not by the tetradrachmum, to which it was equivalent.
(2) Hebrew "ephah" is translated by οἰφί, Egyptian

[1] Most of the instances quoted are taken from Hody, *De Bibliorum Textibus Originalibus*.

pronunciation. This measure still exists among the Copts.

(3) Hebrew "Thummim," translated by ἀλήθεια, the Greek name of the ornament worn by the chief Egyptian judges.

(4) κόνδυ, a special name for a particular kind of Egyptian cup, used in the LXX.

(5) ἄχι, used of anything growing in a marsh—πάπυρος. θίβις = ark in which Moses was exposed.

(6) A numerous class of nouns beginning with the prefix ἀρχι, e.g. ἀρχιμάγειρος, ἀρχισιτοποιός, ἀρχιοινοχόος, ἀρχιδεσμοφύλαξ; cf. in Papyri and Inscrr. ἀρχικύνηγος, ἀρχυπηρέτης. ἀρχι is said to denote simply a court official.

These, of course, are only hints; but when corroborated by the general nature of the version and an unvarying tradition handed down by the oldest Jewish-Greek writers themselves, who had every opportunity of knowing the facts, there is little room for doubt. No one has ever doubted that the translators were *Jews*.

The *raison d'être* of the version is not hard to seek. Besides several very ancient colonies to be found in Egypt, Jews flocked in multitudes to the new city, induced by the splendid opportunity for commercial pursuits, as well as by the kindly disposition of the Egyptian kings and their own less favourable lot in Palestine. Soon we find that Jews occupied some of the highest posts in the whole country. In the natural course of things, half a century or less would see them thoroughly subject at least to the more external influences of their new abode, and none of these could be so powerful as the language commonly spoken, —the language, besides, which was the special medium of their own cherished pursuits. Accordingly, the staple of their ordinary speech would come to be the language of Alexandria. This would be modified by their original dialect of Hebrew or Aramaic, but would gradually approximate to the common vernacular of the city population. Wellhausen,[1] indeed, supposes the existence of a kind of Jewish-Greek jargon, already developed, "which was really Hebrew or Aramaic in disguise," and employs his hypothesis to account for the extreme literalness and frequent harshness of the Septuagint version. But this is a pure hypothesis, and the literalness of the translation is best accounted for on other grounds.

Thus situated, and with their synagogue-worship, which was the very centre of their national life, in full exercise, it must soon come to be the case that many Jews of the generation native to Alexandria, could no longer intelligently follow the reading of the sacred books in their public worship, and the demand would speedily arise for a rendering of, at least, the Law into the language which they could understand. And the great majority of modern scholars hold that these circumstances explain the origin of the Septuagint version. It would be going too far afield to make any particular mention of the peculiar theory of Professor Grätz,[2] who places the first nucleus of the translation about 140 B.C., in the reign of Ptolemy Philometor.

Again it must be noted that the prophetical and poetical books were translated at various times, later than

[1] Art. "Septuagint" in *Encycl. Britann.*
[2] *Geschichte der Juden*, Band iii.

the date of the Pentateuch, and that this was often due, in all probability, to private enterprise. These facts, however, do not affect our investigation of the vocabulary of the LXX., as one hundred and thirty years at most comprise the whole translation, and there is no evidence to show that any part of it was executed outside Alexandria.

In investigating the vocabulary of the LXX. we are investigating the vocabulary of a translation. This translation, moreover, is of a peculiar nature. It is intended to bring out every jot and tittle of the original, because the original is held to be sacred, and not a syllable, therefore, must be lost. Accordingly, the rendering is extraordinarily literal. This implies restriction of vocabulary. But when the range of the collection of writings is so wide, the restriction is scarcely felt. Still, we cannot expect to be able to make the same deductions from what is a rigidly literal translation, as might be looked for in a spontaneous literary product. Further, the translators are Jews. They write in a language whose conceptions are alien to their type of mind. The language is acquired. There must therefore be a certain artificiality of expression, a certain clumsiness both as to forms and structures. Their vocabulary and style cannot fail to show a real Hebraic element, their inheritance from the past. But, apart from this, they are sure to reflect with more or less accuracy the exact type of speech which surrounds them, the particular form of Greek to which they have been first introduced in their everyday dealings with neighbours and traders.

The vocabulary of the LXX. has Attic for its original basis, and so we meet, in ever-varying proportions, with much of the ordinary stock familiar to us in earlier and purer writers. This part of the vocabulary, which is, however, *far less* in proportion to the other elements than the corresponding part of the New Testament vocabulary, we need not for the present dwell upon. It is the common store of most writers in a greater or less degree down to a fairly late date in our era.

But, before discussing the other and far more characteristic elements in the vocabulary of the LXX., it appears to us in place to give a rough analysis of a few chapters taken entirely at random from its pages, which will afford, in brief compass, a general view of its language, and serve as a basis of illustration for the principles in the formation of the vocabulary which have still to be investigated. In the case of the LXX., representative illustrations are specially admissible, seeing that, as a matter of fact, the same elements are found throughout its vocabulary.

We take the first ten chapters of the Book of Deuteronomy, a fair specimen of the ordinary character of the LXX., neither distinguished for special excellence nor special harshness and incorrectness, though perhaps, on the whole, it would fall among the better parts of the work rather than otherwise. Words and forms belonging to the common stock of Greek writers are, of course, unnoticed. The writers are given by whom the word or form is used. When a word in common use is given, it is because of some special sense in the LXX., and those writers alone are quoted who employ it in that sense.

List of Words

α. ἄγονος = barren. Hippoc., Aristot., Theoph., Soph., Plut.
ἀκουστή. Hom., Soph., Eurip. (Isocr.).
ἀκρότομος. Polyb., Philo.
ἀποστήτωσαν. Form.
ἀρσενικός. Very late. Callim., Anthol.
ἀσάλευτος = unmoved. Eurip., Diod., Plut. Adverb in Polyb., N.T.
ἄσηπτος = not liable to rot. Hippoc., Xen.
ἀφάπτω = fasten on. Hdt., Hippoc., Theocr.

β. βαδίζω = go. Colloquial here. So constantly in Comic writers.
βδέλυγμα. Pecul. to LXX. and N.T. Verb in Hippoc., Aristoph., Plut.
βῆμα = treading of sole of foot. Xen., N.T.
(τὰ) βουκόλια. Hdt., Theocr.

γ. γαμβρεύω. Pecul. to LXX. and Josephus.
γνόφος = δνόφος. Only poetical and late prose. N.T.
γραμματοεισαγωγεῖς = Heb. word meaning (1) scribe, (2) magistrate.

δ. δειλιάω. Diod., N.T.
διαγιγνώσκω. Loose use = *memoria revocare*.
διαγογγύζω. N.T.
διανίσταμαι = rise up. Polybius.
διασαφῆσαι. Plato, Polyb., N.T.
διέπεσαν. Form. N.T.
δικαίωμα = ordinance. Peculiar to LXX. and N.T.

ε. ἐγκάθημαι = lie in a place. Polyb., Antiph. Com.
εἶπα. Form. N.T.
ἐκζητέω. Aristid., N.T.
ἐκκλησιάζω. Transitive, Diod.
ἔκφοβος. Aristot., Plut., N.T.
ἐλεημοσύνη = righteousness. N.T.
ἐμπιστεύω = believe.
ἐνάρχομαι = begin (without ritual sense). Polyb., Plut., N.T.

ἐνοπλίζω. Once quoted, Lyc. 205.
ἐνώπιον. N.T.
ἐξολεθρεύω. N.T.
ἐπαναστρέφω = (simply) return.
εὔκληρος = fortunate. Anthol., Suid. εὐκλήρημα in Antiph. Com.
εὐμήκης = tall. Plato, Theocr.
ἐφοδεύω. Late. In Xen. Cyr. 8. 6. 16, of an officer who visited annually the satrapies of Persia. Timocl. Com.

ζ. ζωγρεία = Heb. word for "survivor." In Hdt., Polyb., Strabo = one taken alive.

η. ἤλθατε. Form. N.T.
ἤλθοσαν. Form. N.T.

θ. θηλυκός. Very late. Dion. Hal.
θύελλα. Entirely poetical. N.T.
θυμόω. Passive form. Scarcely in prose. N.T.
ἴδοσαν. Form. N.T.
ἱερατεύω. Herodn., Inscrr., N.T.

κ. καιρός = χρόνος. Late. N.T.
κάμινος. Hdt., Aesch., Galen., N.T.
καταλέω = grind down. Hom., Hdt., Hippoc., Strabo.
κατασκοπεύω (= κατασκοπέω). Xen., Polyb., Plut.
καταφυτεύω = plant. Plut., Lucian.
κατισχύω = encourage. Dion. Hal. = strengthen; N.T. = prevail.
καύχημα. Pindar, Lesbonax, N.T.
κιβωτός. Aristoph., Lysias, and late writers; N.T.
κοιτάζομαι = go to bed. Pind., Polyb.
κόπος. Late in prose = trouble, burden. Poetry and N.T.
κόσμος = Heb. word for "heavenly hosts as ornaments of the heavens."
κράταιος. Poet. Only late prose. Plut., etc.; N.T.
κρῖμα. Polyb., N.T.
κτῆνος. Hdt., Hom., Xen., N.T.

λ. λάκκος = cistern. Hdt., Aristoph., Xen. (Demos.).
λαξεύω. Eumath. (λάξευσις. Schol. ad Theocr.; λαξευτός, N.T.).

λατρεύω = serve God. N.T. Used by Eurip. = serve the gods.
λιμαγχονέω = reduce by hunger. Hippoc., Antisth. ap. Stob.
μ. μακροημερεύω. Peculiar to LXX.
μαλακία = sickness. Vit. Hom., N.T.
ν. νάπη. Poet., Hdt., Xen.
ο. ὁδηγέω = Pseud.-Phocyl., Hippoc., Aesch., Eur., N.T. All = lead.
οἰκτίρμων. Theocr., Anth., N.T.
ὀλιγοστός = one out of a few. Plut.
ὅραμα. Aristot., Xen., Aristid., N.T.
ὀχυρός = strong (military term). Xen., Polyb.
⌐ π. παιδίσκη = slave. Late. But Menander. N.T.
παῖς = slave. Tragg., Comm., late prose, N.T.
παραπορεύομαι. Polyb., N.T.
παρεμβολή. Polyb., N.T., Theophil. *Com.*; Crito *Com.*; Diphil.
πατάσσω = kill. Late. N.T.
περιούσιος. N.T. fr. περιουσία = property (περίειμι = have over and above).
πλάξ = flat stone. Lucian, N.T.
πληθύνω = increase (trans.), N.T.
ποιήσαισαν. Form.
πολεμιστής. Poetic word.
πολυπλασιάζω. Plut., Herodn.
πολυπληθέω. Pecul. to LXX.
πολυχρονίζω. Pecul. to LXX.
προνομεύω = plunder. Dion. H. often, Polyb., Plut., Posidip. *Com.*
⌐ πρόσκειμαι. Used of devotion to God. So in Dion. Cass. and Epictet.
προσόχθισμα. Pecul. to LXX. Verb in Orac. Sibyll. and N.T.
πρότερος ἡμῶν. Scarcely in earlier lang.; cf. John 1. 15, πρῶτός μου ἦν.
πτερωτός. Hdt., Tragg., Plut. (once in Plato).
πτήσσω. Scarcely in prose. Poet. word.

πτωχία. Late form.
ρ. ῥῆμα = thing. N.T.
σ. σκληροκαρδία. N.T.
σκληροτράχηλος. N.T.
σκληρύνω. Metaph., N.T. Ord. sense in Hippoc Aristot.
σκῶλον = snare. Etym. M. and Hesych. = σκῶλος, pointed stake; cf. σκωλοῦμαι in Aquila = be offended.
συγκυρῶ = be adjacent. Polyb., Plut.
συνάντησις. Eurip., Dion. H., Plut., N.T.
συνεκπολεμέω. Diod.
συντρίβω. Pass = be beaten. Polyb., Plut., N.T.
τ. τειχήρης = fortified. In this sense only in LXX.
τροφοφορέω. N.T., Apocr.
τυλόω = swell. In Hdt., Xen., Theocr. = grow hard.
υ. ὑπόστασις = Heb. word for "burden." Almost = etymol. sense of Latin "*sustentatio.*"
ὑποστέλλω = shrink from. Hippoc., Dinarch., N.T.
φ. φάγεσθε. Form.
φλιαί = doorposts. Hom., Bion, Polyb., Theocr.
φονευτής. Byzantine writers.
ψ. ψωμίζω = feed. Aristoph., Hippoc., N.T.

A rough analysis of this short index of the more uncommon words in the first ten chapters of Deuteronomy gives the following results. Of 110 words and forms examined—

      50 occur in the New Testament.
      17 „ „ Polybius.
      16 „ „ the Tragedians.
      15 „ „ Plutarch.
      12 „ „ Comic writers.
      10 „ „ Hippocrates.
      10 „ „ Herodotus.
      10 „ „ Xenophon.

While 16 are peculiar to the Septuagint.

We have given this short analysis because it can be

so easily illustrated from the index above; but a wider view of the facts will be gained if the results of an examination of the whole Book of Deuteronomy, comprising thirty-four chapters, be presented. It will be found that the inferences which can be deduced from the investigation of the restricted area are precisely corroborated by the more extended inquiry. Both bring to light definite elements, which form the determining factors in the vocabulary of the LXX.

DEUTERONOMY—CHAPS. I.–XXXIV

Of 313 Words examined—

37 per cent.	116 occur in the New Testament.
16 ,,	51 ,, ,, Plutarch.
14 ,,	43 ,, ,, the Tragedians.
13 ,,	42 ,, ,, Xenophon.
13 ,,	41 ,, ,, Polybius.
12 ,,	39 ,, ,, Comic writers.
12 ,,	38 ,, ,, Herodotus.
10 ,,	33 ,, ,, Hippocrates.
7 ,,	c. 20 ,, ,, Diodorus.
5 ,,	c. 17 ,, ,, Plato.
5 ,,	c. 17 ,, ,, Philo.
11 ,,	36 are peculiar to the Septuagint.

These tables are suggestive in various directions.

(1.) In the first place, an important and interesting element in the vocabulary of the LXX. is that which consists of words belonging to the old Greek literature as represented by the Tragedians and poets like Homer and Pindar. These have fallen into abeyance in the most flourishing period of Attic prose, and now emerge again into the light. The history of this process is hard to trace. It seems by no means unlikely that many of the words, though confined to a particular type of literature within the compass of our knowledge, really formed part of the regular vocabulary in particular regions, and may have been in constant use on the lips of the people. Of course, it *is* possible that, merely through the general mixture of dialects which took place, and the loss of that refined sensibility which distinguished instinctively between what was adapted for poetry and for prose respectively, the words passed somewhat rapidly into the ordinary store of words. But the former seems the more probable hypothesis, and it is easy to see that the facts which it supposes do not exclude, but are rendered more plausible by the grounds alleged for the alternative supposition.

Many instances occur in the lists: *e.g.*—

ἀσάλευτος. A poetical adjective in Euripides.
γνόφος. Not in good prose.
θύελλα. A thoroughly poetical word.
καύχημα. Apparently almost peculiar to Pindar.
κόπος. Never in early prose.
πτερωτός. Good instance of thoroughly poetical adjective.

As it happens, *Homeric* words are scantily represented in the tables; but in many parts of the LXX. which we have examined, as, for instance, 1 Samuel, they are extraordinarily frequent.

(2.) Another striking characteristic of the stock of words exhibited by the LXX. is the well-marked Ionic strain represented by terms which appear chiefly in Hippocrates and Herodotus. It is difficult to give an entirely satisfying reason for this phenomenon. We have no definite information as to the relation between Asiatic Greek and that of Alexandria. Necessarily, this would be intimate. There may in all probability have been an old literary tradition which became a kind of standard for the Greeks of the coast of Asia Minor, based on the earlier Ionic literature. The Ionic literary language would originally be the popular speech purified, so to speak, and stereotyped. So that all along, a close connection would exist, as at Athens, between the spoken and the written languages. But after literary production had ceased, its particular type of speech would remain a powerful influence in moulding the ordinary language. In some such fashion as this, we may believe, the words under consideration became part of the spoken vocabulary of the maritime Greeks of Asia Minor, and in due course, through commercial communication and the other customary modes of intercourse, found their way into the word-store of the Jews of Alexandria.

The following examples are from the lists:—

    ἀφάπτω = fasten on. In Herod. and Hippoc. with the interesting addition of Theocritus, an Alexandrian writer.

    βουκόλια. Hdt. (again in company with Theocritus).

    καταλέω = grind down. Hdt. Hippocr. (also in Homer).

    λιμαγχονέω. Hippocr. (Frag. of Antisthenes).

    τυλόω. Hdt. (also in Theocritus and Xen.).

    ὑποστέλλω = shrink from. Hippocr. (also in Dinarchus, a Corinthian).

Many other instances could be given from the larger group of words.

(3.) As might be expected from what has been said in a former part of this dissertation, many affinities with the language of Xenophon are to be found. This is the natural result of the growth of the tendency to laxness in observing the strict boundaries of correct prose, combined with ever-increasing foreign influences.

Examples from our list are—

ἄσηπτος = not liable to rot. Xen. (also in Hippocr.).
βῆμα = the tread of the foot.
κατασκοπεύω (= κατασκοπέω). First in Xen.
κτῆνος. Good instance of a thoroughly poetical word, brought into prose by Xen.
νάπη. Another term of the same class, etc. etc.

(4.) This last class can scarcely be separated from a very large list of words which the LXX. has in common with the writers of the "Common" dialect, in short, with the literary language which arose in the period which gave it birth. This class, of course, is far wider in range than any of those already glanced at, as it really embraces all the outstanding peculiarities of the later literary language. And, without doubt, the LXX. comes far nearer the literature of the ".Common Dialect" in actual vocabulary than in style, or syntax, or general tone. The fact is interesting as showing that it was easier for the literary men to model the structure of their sentences after the great masters of literature than to preserve their vocabulary, even by artificial means. Still, writers like Polybius and Plutarch show a far more intimate relation to Plato and Aristotle, even in vocabulary, than they do towards the LXX.

It is impossible, within our limits, even to indicate the numerous points of contact between the vocabulary of the LXX. and that of the writers of the κοινή. A few hints must suffice. Many of the points of contact referred to come under the head of the classes already examined. Polybius, Diodorus, Strabo, Philo, and Plutarch all exhibit the characteristics looked at under (1), (2), and (3) of this section.

But there are additional features. Perhaps the most important of these is one common to the immature and the decaying stages of a language. This is the habit of forming compounds. As Rutherford well points out (*New Phryn.* p. 6): "Before a language is matured, and that feeling of language developed which sees in a common word the most suitable expression for a common action or fact, there is a tendency to make work-a-day words more expressive by compounding with a preposition." In illustration, he quotes from Sophocles a long list of compounds, especially with the preposition ἐκ, ἐξ, as ἐξανέχεσθαι, ἐξελευθεροστομεῖν, ἐξατιμάζειν, and many others, which differ in no way from the uncompounded verbs, except in having a touch of vividness or picturesqueness added.

The same tendency displays itself in the later language in a greatly intensified degree and harsher forms. But now it is because language has lost its concentrated force. Words adequate enough to express the intended meaning have become weakened to the popular imagination. They are felt to be too vague just because simplicity is so. The artificiality of language becomes the reflection of artificiality of thought. It is imagined that by heaping on prepositions or other elements to a word it gains in content. The examples are partly from the list and partly taken at random—

διανίσταμαι = stand up. Polyb. (no meaning added).
διασκορπίζω = (practically) σκορπίζω. Polyb.
ἐμπεριπατέω = walk, or, walk about. Philo.
ἐνάρχομαι = simple ἄρχομαι. Polyb., Plut.
καταδυναστεύω = δυναστεύω. Plut., Diod.
καταστρατοπεδεύω = στρατοπεδεύω. Polyb.
καταφυτεύω = φυτεύω. Plut.
παραπορεύομαι. Usu. = simple "go." Polyb. etc. etc.
προσεκκαίω. Dion. Cass.
συνεκπολεμέω. Diod.

There is also an inclination to form new compounds, such as—

ἀκρότομος. Polyb., Philo.
ἐγκάθημαι. Polyb.
ἐμπιστεύω. Plut., Polyb.
νευροκοπέω. Polyb., Strabo.
πολυπλασιάζω. Plut.
προνομεύω. Plut., Polyb., Dion. Hal.
συμβολοκοπέω. Philo, etc. etc.

We purposely omit, for the present, the consideration of the two chief remaining elements in our tables of results, viz. the batch of words which the vocabulary of the LXX. has in common with the New Testament, and also those peculiar to itself, as these must be treated later on with greater fulness and minuteness than belongs to our present rough analysis.

(5.) The store of words on which the LXX. draws is enriched further by a very interesting class of terms which may be called "vernacular." A large number of expressions which have evidently long been current in the speech of the people, including almost certainly the Athenian populace, appear now in the written language. They belong to that "oral tradition" which Professor

THE SEPTUAGINT 39

Jebb describes[1] as "preceding the ancient literature of Greece, coexisting with it and surviving it." It was inevitable that they should find a place in the LXX., which is so much a transcript of the spoken language.

EXAMPLES

βρέχω = ὕειν, βροχή = ὑετός. The verb occurs in this sense in Telecl. *Com.* (Mein. 2. 376). Phrynichus, 258, holds that the verb in this sense is entirely to be rejected. Lobeck considers that the word, originally poetical, became vulgarised after the palmy days of Greek literature, and so is found in Polybius, Arrian, the LXX., and N.T. So βροχή, found in Geoponica, ii. 39, and Eustathius, as well as the LXX. and N.T. Also ἀβροχία in Josephus and Philo. It seems more likely that, at an early date, these words passed into the colloquial vocabulary; and it is suggestive, in this connection, to find that βροχή is a modern Greek term for "rain."

γλωσσόκομον. Phryn. says on γλωττοκομεῖον· ἐπὶ μόνου τοῦ τῶν αὐλητικῶν γλωττῶν ἀγγείου. ὕστερον δὲ καὶ εἰς ἑτέραν χρῆσιν κατεσκευάζετο, βιβλίων ἢ ἱματίων ἢ ἀργύρου ἢ ὁτουοῦν ἄλλου· καλοῦσι δ' αὐτὸ οἱ ἀμαθεῖς γλωσσόκομον.
The word is found in the Comic poets, Timocles (Mein. 3. 590) and Apollodorus Carystius (Mein. 4. 444), in the simple sense of a box or case. This was evidently its popular meaning, which is found also in Plut., Joseph., and N.T.

γογγύζω, γογγυσμός. Phryn. brands these words as Ionian, and is only acquainted in literature with περιγογγύζω, used by Phocylides. The correct expressions, he asserts, are τονθορύζειν and τονθορυσμός. Nunnesius, quoted by Lobeck, says: "Pollux τὸ γογγύζειν tribuit columbis quibus auctor Philomelae et turdis

[1] *Handbook to Modern Greek*, by Vincent and Dickson, Appendix, p. 289.

gemere assignat." But the noun occurs in Anaxandrides' *Com.* (Mein. 3. 174).

The words are frequent in the N.T. = murmur, murmuring. It seems, therefore, legitimate to assume that at an early date they belonged to the vernacular.

κειρία = cord or band. Aristoph. *Av.* 816, where the Schol. says: κειρία· εἶδος ζώνης ἐκ σχοινίων, παρεοικὸς ἱμάντι ᾗ δεσμοῦσι τὰς κλίνας. Sept., N.T., and Plut. Evidently a vernacular word, which has all along formed part of the popular language.

κοίτων = Attic δωμάτιον. (Poll. 10. 43, also quotes προκοιτῶν.) Aristoph. *Frag.* (Mein. 2. 947). The word is censured by Menander (Mein. 4. 314), a fact proving that it was in common currency at that time. Athenaeus gives a Fragment from Matron, the writer of parodies (c. 370 B.C.), in which the word occurs. Several times in LXX. and late writers, also N.T. Inscr. Delos (130 B.C.): ἐπὶ τοῦ κοιτῶνος τῆς βασιλίσσης (Dittenberger, 244. 5).

λυχνία. Phryn. 289: ἀντὶ τούτου λυχνίον λέγε. And in his Appendix, p. 50: λυχνίον· οἱ ἀμαθεῖς λυχνίαν αὐτὸ καλοῦσι. So Pollux, 10. 115 (quoted by Lobeck), says that λυχνίον is "vulgarly" called λυχνία. It was clearly a word in regular circulation, and probably from an early date. Cf. Inscr. Ieronda (240 B.C.): τήν τε λυχνίαν τὴν μεγάλην (Ditt. 170. 13).

ὀθόνιον = linen cloth, in plur. = stripes of linen. Several times in Hippocr., Aristoph. *Frag.* (Mein. 2. 989). Several times in LXX. and N.T.

ὀνυχίζω = pare the nails, or metaph., examine minutely. Cratin. (Mein. 2. 214). Aristoph. *Frag.* (Mein. 2. 1217), on which Suidas: ὀνυχίζεται· ἀκριβολογεῖται, οὕτως Ἀριστοφάνης. Evidently a colloquial word which the translators of the O.T. used to express the cloven hoof.

παιδίσκη. Phryn. 216: παιδίσκῃ· τοῦτο ἐπὶ τῆς θεραπαίνης οἱ νῦν τιθέασιν, οἱ δ' ἀρχαῖοι ἐπὶ τῆς νεάνιδος. Prof. Jebb on Lys. *Or.* I. 11, 12, regards θεράπαινα and παιδισκή

in that passage as synonymous. So, too, Isaeus, viii. 35:
ἀνδράποδα ... καὶ δύο θεραπαίνας καὶ παιδισκήν, where
there seems little distinction, though perhaps the latter,
as Schömann (quoted by Jebb) suggests, has less menial
work to do. More likely it is a term adopted from the
vernacular which had fixed to the word παιδισκή the
meaning of "slave," just as Scotch servants almost
invariably use the word "girl" technically of those who
are in their own position. In the later Greek, this
signification is exceedingly frequent. So in Inscrr.,
e.g. one of Delphi, 178 B.C.: Ἀσανδρος ... ἀνάτιθησι
τῶι Ἀπόλλωνι τῶι Πυθιωι ἐλευθέραν ... Εὐπορίαν τὴν
αὑτοῦ παιδισκήν (Ditt. 451. 4).

στρῆνος = strength (usu. in a bad sense, of strength which
is eager to gratify itself lawlessly). Except a single
instance in Nicostratus *Com.* B.C. 300 (Mein. 5. 84), the
word is not found till Lycophron and the LXX. Pollux
(quoted by Rutherford, p. 476) says that Callias, the
Comic poet (c. 412 B.C.), used the compound στρηνό-
φωνος = loud-voiced. Also, the verb στρηνιᾶν is found
in Antiph. *Com.* (c. 387), Sophilus (c. 350?), and
Diphilus (320). These various instances appear
to us to show, as conclusively as anything could,
that the word must have existed in the colloquial
vocabulary from the earliest times, and found its
way into the LXX. just for this reason. Also in
N.T.

τρύβλιον. Found, curiously, in Hippoc. as a special
measure used in medical prescriptions. But this pre-
supposes its earlier existence in something very like the
sense of "cup," "dish," in which it appears in Aristoph. *Achar.* 278, *Av.* 77. So that we may well believe
it belonged in this sense to the current popular speech
in very early days, though its use in books did not become frequent till the later stages of the language, in
the LXX., N.T., Plut. etc. etc.

φιμόω = compress. Aristoph. *Nub.* 592. Not found again
till the LXX. and N.T. The reason probably is that

it was a word of common life, not considered admissible into literary works.

χάρτης = paper. This word used to be supposed by some scholars to be derived from Aramaic. Of course, the converse is the case, as it is found in Plato *Com.* Frag. 10, and Cebes, Tab. 4. Thayer also quotes Kirchhoff, Inscrr. Attic. I. no. 324 (dated 407 B.C.). It was clearly a vernacular word, which disappears, so far as literature is concerned, till we find it again in the LXX. and N.T.

These are specimens of a number of instances collected.

(6.) Another link which binds the language of the LXX. to the early vernacular speech is the large number of diminutives which are to be found in its vocabulary. This is a distinct element in its composition, and the interesting point about it is that a great proportion of those diminutives are to be found in the Comic writers of an early date, the very authors who would be expected to shed light, in a special degree, on the colloquial language of their time.

It need scarcely be said that many of the diminutives in the LXX. have lost their particular sense, and are used as exact equivalents of the words from which they have been formed. We give some instances—

ἀρνίον. Eubul. (M. 3. 212, 268), Philippid. (M. 4. 476).
βαλάντιον. Telecl. (M. 2. 371), Aristoph. (M. 2. 982, 1165).
κεράμιον. Alexid. (M. 3. 409), Men. (M. 4. 133), Eubul. (M. 3. 26), Antiph. (M. 3. 141), Aristoph. (M. 2. 1186).
κοράσιον. Philippid. (M. 4. 497).
ὀπήτιον. Nicostr. (M. 2. 844).
παιδάριον. Eleven instances in Meineke.
σανδάλιον. Men. (M. 4. 317), Antiph. (M. 3. 153), Cratin. (M. 2. 91), Cephis. (M. 2. 884), Theoph. (M. 2. 809).
στηθύνιον. Eubul. (ap. Athen. 2. 65 c.).
στρουθίον. Anaxand. (M. 3. 164), Ephipp. (M. 3. 326).

σχοίνιον. (Chiefly Comic.) Four exx. in Meineke.
φορτίον. Eight instances in Meineke.
χαλκίον. Ten instances in Meineke.

(7.) Marked characteristics of the vocabulary of the LXX. are its formation of new verbs, with a special tendency towards forms in -όω, -εύω, -άζω -ίζω, and its modifications in the use of existing ones to suit its own purpose.

Examples

(a) ἀναθεματίζω, ἐκτοκίζω, ἐνωτίζομαι, σαββατίζω, ὀρθρίζω, σπερματίζω, ἐκμυκτηρίζω.
ἐνκαινίζω, ἐνταφίαζω.
ἀποδεκατεύω, ἐξολεθρεύω, ἐπιγαμβρεύω, μακροημερεύω, πρωτοτοκεύω.
ἀποπεμπτόω, ἀτεκνόω, ἐκριζόω, ἐνδυναμόω, παραζηλόω. ἐνδοξάζω κ.τ.λ.

(b) Transitive verbs[1] receive an intransitive sense: *e.g.* καταπαύω, κατισχύω, κορέννυμι.
Intransitive verbs receive a transitive sense: *e.g.* αὐταρκέω, ἐξαίρω, κατασπεύδω.
περιβιόω = keep alive. ζωογονέω = *vivifico*.

(8.) One of the specially noteworthy features of the language of the LXX. has still to be pointed out, and that is the large admixture of foreign words which can be traced in its vocabulary.

1. The chief element under this head is, of course, the Hebrew. But as it has to be examined minutely in immediate connection with the New Testament, it is needless to anticipate here. For the sake of completeness, however, we may summarise briefly.

[1] These instances are taken from H. G. Thiersch, *De Pentateuchi Versione Alexandrina*, p. 99.

A. Actual Hebrew words occur in the LXX. in various guises—

(a) Hebrew words in Greek letters: *e.g.* πάσχα, σαβαώθ, χερουβείν.
(b) Words which have become Greek through the addition of regular Greek endings: *e.g.* γέεννα, βάτος, κόρος.
(c) Words which have undergone certain modifications: *e.g.* σάββατον, σίκλος, σίκερα, ὕσσωπος.

B. Words formed on the model of existing Hebrew words or expressions—

(a) *Nouns*: as, ἐφημερία, ὁλοκαύτωμα, παντοκράτωρ, παραπικρασμός, ῥαντισμός, σκληροκαρδία κ.τ.λ.
(b) *Adjectives*: as, ἀνθρωπάρεσκος, ἀπερίτμητος, πρωτότοκος, σκληροτράχηλος, ταπεινόφρων κ.τ.λ.
(c) *Verbs*: as, ἀναθεματίζω, ἀποδεκατεύω, βεβηλόω, πληροφορέω κ.τ.λ.

C. Greek words modified by the influence of Hebrew conceptions—

(a) *Ordinary terms*: *e.g.* ἔθνος, εἴδωλον, ἐκκλησία, γραμματεύς, στρατιά κ.τ.λ.
ἐξομολογέω, παιδεύω, πατάσσω κ.τ.λ.
(b) *Theological and religious terms*: *e.g.* ἄγγελος, διάβολος, εἰρήνη, κύριος, παιδεία, σωτηρία.
δικαιόω, ἐκλέγομαι, πορνεύω, φωτίζω.

All these classes will be examined and illustrated carefully further on in the Dissertation.

2. Words from other languages—

(a) *Egyptian*: κόνδυ, θίβις, ξύθος, βάρις, πάπυρος, σινδών κ.τ.λ.
(b) *Cyrenaic*: βουνός. This asserted by Hdt. 4. 199; Valckenaer on Hdt. 4. 351 (quoted by Lobeck, *Phryn.* 356)—"Vox Cyrenaicis usitata; a Dori-

ensibus in Sicilia vocem transsumsisse videtur Aeschylus. A Cyrenaicis accipere potuerunt Alexandrini; recentiores Graeci quivis colles et tumulos βουνούς dixerunt." And Carr (on Luke 3. 5) well remarks: "It (*i.e.* βουνός) is an interesting trace of the connection between the Jews and Cyrene, which, next to Alexandria, contained the largest Jewish population of any African city."

(c) *Macedonian* (?): παρεμβολή, ῥυμή.
(d) *Persian*: γάζα = treasure; κίδαρις = tiara; μανδύη = a special part of Persian armour.
(e) *Cilician*: σισόη. Hesych. says that this was a particular kind of tonsure with the inhabitants of Phaselis, a Cilician town.

This table of foreign words must be taken, in the case of some of the terms, with reservation, as the old authorities may often have had the most slender of grounds for referring an uncouth word to a particular foreign tongue.

CHAPTER V

BRIEF SURVEY OF THE MAIN FACTS IN THE HISTORY OF THE VOCABULARY OF GREEK LITERATURE, FROM THE COMPLETION OF THE SEPTUAGINT (ABOUT 200–160 B.C.) DOWN TO C. 100 A.D.

ROUGHLY speaking, an interval of about two hundred years separates the New Testament from the Septuagint. In most languages a period of that duration would mean great modifications and many new developments. It is different with the two centuries we are considering. Two types of speech have become stereotyped, and have both been used in literature. The one, indeed, is only a literary language; for this purpose it has been formed, and its aim is to keep itself as free as possible from accommodation to the popular standard. The other is originally the common speech of the people; but, after passing through the mould of Hebrew thought, it, too, has become, in a sense, literary, or at least it has become the vehicle of a large and uniquely important collection of books. That has given fixity to it, so that henceforward it may be used as a standard or norm.

Strangely enough, this "Hellenistic" type of Greek cannot be said to be found again until, for the second time, a group of writers whose modes of thinking are predominantly Hebrew, give it currency in a more influential form than ever, through the collection of works which make up the New Testament. There are breaks, so to speak, in this long interval of silence. That cluster of writings which form a kind of appendix to the Old Testament and a prologue to the New, which, for want of a better designation, are termed "Apocrypha," must, we think, be regarded as belonging, in point of language, both to the Hellenic type of the "Common" dialect, and in a much less degree to the "Hellenistic" of the LXX.

The greater part of them is, in all likelihood, the work of Jewish writers; yet these are imbued with Greek influences, and especially with Greek conceptions, to an extent which places them in a quite distinct sphere from that in which the writers of the LXX. move. So that it is perhaps advisable to glance at their characteristics, as regards vocabulary, in the same line of development as the authors of the "Common" dialect. A brief survey of some of the distinguishing features of these authors, in the particular province of "vocabulary," should place us at a better point of view for estimating the language of the New Testament, and the influences which moulded it.

As has been already noted, those writers after the days of Alexander who were conscious of a real literary impulse, created for themselves a special type of literary speech. The "Common" dialect, therefore, is not a mere vague reflection of the mixed language prevailing all round the shores of the Mediterranean. It is differentiated from that by several distinct characteristics. For one thing, the writers who employ it are cultivated men. They have received a polite education. They write not only for the purpose of giving information to the public regarding certain important or interesting subjects, but also with the sense of the worth of literature as itself educative. Certainly they aim, above all things, at clearness of statement and plainness of speech, but they never exhibit that entire artlessness of language which marks the Hellenistic writers. The latter are, one may say, unconscious of their vocabulary. Lucidity is their one aim. The writers of the κοινή have not lost entirely the sense for effect. So they choose their words, and even seem to lay down definite principles for themselves as to their mode of selection. They have studied, and know the great masterpieces of earlier times. The influence of these cannot be disregarded. They are aware that literary prose has reached a definite level in the past. Accordingly, the standard once attained will have, in any case, an unconscious effect on their work. But to counterbalance their culture and education, and even their innate feeling for literature (for it may be presumed that in this they surpass their contemporaries), stands a long array of unfavourable conditions. They cannot escape their environment. They are surrounded by mixed populations, whose dialects comprise words and phrases and forms borrowed from every variety of Greek. The separate provinces in which they were born and brought up have each its peculiar type of language. Local colouring prevails all round. And common to all of them is the original corrupted Attic which forms the basis of the new cosmopolitan Greek. Besides, vigorous national life, that life which kept the earlier Attic pure and forcible, and which afforded so keen a stimulus to thought that only a refined and subtle tongue could express the conceptions of the great thinkers,—that life has given place to a spurious, relaxed existence which calls forth a corresponding artificial language. And so the striking fact comes to light that these writers, although they are acquainted with the wide and expressive and pure vocabulary of the Golden Age, are really unfit to use it. The great, fruitful ideas of the past, nourished by the pride and glory of Athens, have made room for meagre, thin conceptions which reflect themselves in the language. Therefore we find that the writers of the κοινή use only an excerpt from the Attic vocabulary. This they supplement by recent formations, sometimes due to the general tendencies underlying the speech of the time, sometimes the result of special local idiosyncrasies.

After all, however, their dialect, which in its main features is common to them all, stands high above the speech of popular intercourse. It is therefore artificial, with a real effort after literary effect. We can only glance at representatives of the κοινή in respect of Vocabulary, paying special regard to those who may be expected to throw light of some kind on our subject.

Polybius.—Polybius, the earliest outstanding writer of this " dialect," is also a very typical one. His plain, matter-of-fact style appears at first sight to be very much on the level of the popular language. But closer scrutiny modifies our view. Certainly he does give us glimpses of the colloquial speech, but his vocabulary is predominantly literary.

It cannot be said that he shows many peculiarities.

No doubt we do come across words like συντερμονέω, καταπλαγής, ἐκπαθής, and others, which apparently are only found in him; and also particular uses, as σύνταξις = narrative; ὀφθαλμιάω = be envious, etc. etc.; also favourite words, like πραγματικός (of which Schweighäuser gives at least forty instances in various senses): but speaking generally, his vocabulary seems very representative of the κοινή, and keeps on a uniform level. Perhaps the leading element in it is a striking kinship with Aristotle's stock of words. One cause of this, in all probability, is the philosophical cast of Polybius' own mind, which naturally leads him to use a terminology already laid to his hand, though he cannot fail to do so with a certain laxity and inaccuracy. So he constantly employs terms like θεώρημα, σωματοειδής, πρόθεσις, κινητικός, ἐπανόρθωσις, ἀπόρημα, and the like, which have a more or less philosophical colouring. Seeing that his tendency is somewhat prosaic, we should not expect, nor do we find, the poetic element of the κοινή so strong in him. Still, thoroughly poetical words come up here and there, such as ἀτρεκής, γεφυρόω, εὐθαρσής, προτροπάδην, etc. etc., which prove that this is a fixed characteristic of the language of the period, and forms part of the general stock of words.

Of later writers, Plutarch appears to be the one with whom he has most points of contact. Yet this is less important, because these points of contact occur, not in any peculiar phase or type of diction, but rather in the common basis of the dialect which they both use. They seem to agree especially in carrying on the particular tradition of Aristotle and his contemporaries.

But Polybius is an author who does throw light on the vocabularies both of Septuagint and New Testament. It is interesting, however, to find that this is, as a rule, where these agree. In other words, Polybius is, at such times, employing the colloquial language of his day. In a rough examination made of a part of Book I. of his *Histories*, about 18 per cent. of his vocabulary was to be found in the LXX. and New Testament. Polybius constantly displays the want of flexible phraseology. And this calls forth a number of new formations which are, in general, common to him along with Diodorus, Strabo, Philo, Plutarch, and Pausanias. Indeed, it is these additions to the Lexicon which give individual tone to the several authors of the κοινή. The products of this artificial gift of invention are usually verbal forms, which strive, by means of accumulation of elements, to restore to words the force they have lost. So in Polybius we meet with forms like προσεπιζητέω, προσεπιμετρέω, προσεπιφθέγγομαι, προσκατατάσσω, διεξικνέομαι, ἐπιδιασαφέω, ἐπιδιατείνω, etc. etc., in almost all of which one of the prepositions adds nothing whatever to the conception. But as we touched on this point in connection with the LXX., it is needless to dwell on it again. On the whole, it may be pronounced the most outstanding characteristic of the later language.

Apocrypha.—It may appear anomalous, at this stage and in this historical succession, to introduce some brief remarks on the vocabulary of the Apocrypha, but while these are Jewish works, they are not so in the sense of the LXX. and New Testament. Their true place seems to be between the writings of Philo and a book like the

Epistle to the Hebrews. That is to say, they are distinctly Alexandrian, but have, so far as vocabulary and style are concerned, assimilated Greek influence to such an extent that their language, with slight exceptions, is cultivated Greek, which can be placed on the level of the writers of the κοινή. And, roughly speaking, they may be dated between Polybius and Philo. The various books cannot, indeed, be regarded as all occupying the same position. Between 3 *Maccabees*, for example, and 2 *Maccabees* there is a vast difference, so far as concerns pure expression and mastery of the language of culture. On the other hand, there are many resemblances and even common peculiarities which lead us to class them together. All the books contain Hebraisms, but this with far greater restrictions than the LXX. or New Testament. Thus 2 *Maccabees*, while containing Hebrew usages as ἀδελφοί = fellow-countrymen, and a few more, shows a great partiality for combinations like αὐτὸς αὐτόθι, ἄγειν ἀγῶνα, δυσφόρως φέρειν, εὐμένειαν ... δυσμένειαν κ.τ.λ., which manifest both a certain mastery of the language and a sense of literary effect superior to Hellenistic writers. This book also has frequent coincidences with Polybius. Instances are: ἀναζυγή, retreat (of an army); ἐναπερείδεσθαι, to bring down (anger or vengeance) violently on some one; καταπειράζειν, make an attempt on the enemy, etc. etc.

Several of these works, notably the *Wisdom of Solomon* and 2 *Maccabees*, show their thoroughly Greek character in their varied power of expression, and the rich store of appropriate words they have at command, a fact which comes out especially in the numerous

SURVEY OF THE MAIN FACTS

parallelisms and antitheses which they delight to employ. The "Wisdom" contains technical expressions of Platonic and Stoic philosophy, as: ὕλη ἄμορφος, πνεῦμα νοερόν, πρόνοια κ.τ.λ. Assonances and paronomasia are also common in it, as: προσδοσία . . . προσδοκία, ἰδίας ἰδιότητος, εὐώδωσε . . . διώδευσαν . . . Perhaps what chiefly strikes one in their vocabularies is the immense number of peculiar words, often ἅπαξ λεγόμενα, which are to be found there: *e.g.*—

δυσπέτημα, δεξιάζεσθαι, εὐγενίζειν, ὁπλολογεῖν τινα.
πολεμοτροφεῖν, προσπυροῦν, διάσταλσις.
πεφρενωμένος = in high spirits; διεξάγειν = behave; ἐκλύειν = depart.
πάνσοφος, παγγέωργος, ἐπικαρπολογεῖσθαι.
ἐπιρραψογεῖσθαι, μαλακοψυχεῖν, ἐθνοπλήκτος.
ὁμοζηλία, ὀροφοκοιτεῖν, ὑπερασπιστρία, ῥεμβασμός,
κακόμοχθος, νηπιοκτόνος, εἰδέχθεια.[1]

We have given all these instances, partly to show the alarming proportion in which the Greek vocabulary was increasing even among cultivated writers, and all the time in a diffuse and inelegant direction, and partly to point out a tendency which was strongly at work in the LXX., and which appears inseparable from Jewish use of Greek, that of forming cumbrous and uncouth compounds on the model of Hebrew expressions, rather than conveying the thought more flexibly by broken-up phrases.

Philo.—We omit Diodorus and Strabo as sufficiently represented by Polybius, and glance next at Philo, who, in respect of vocabulary, is one of the most interesting

[1] These lists are compiled from the large collections in the Introductions to Grimm's *Handbücher zu den Apocryphen*.

of the writers of the "Common" dialect. He is all the more important for our subject as being a true Jew, a native of Alexandria, and a voluminous Greek writer. But his language is entirely different in general character from the so-called dialect of Alexandria. No doubt he does employ some words which are considered peculiar to that type of speech, such as ἀμφιάζεσθαι, καμμύειν, ἐμπιστεύειν, and a few more; but these are exceptional, and in any case we could not expect him to be unaffected by the direct influences of his surroundings.

Philo's tendencies of thought brought him into the closest connection with Greek philosophy, made him indeed an enthusiast for Plato, and so we need not be surprised to find that Plato became his master in the use of language as well as his ideal of a philosopher. This gave rise to the well-known saying: ἢ Πλάτων φιλωνίζει ἢ Φίλων πλατωνίζει. Siegfried has put together a list of over three hundred rare words which are to be found in both authors. These are by no means chiefly philosophical terms, but belong to every phase of the language. It is interesting to observe that Philo, though thoroughly proud of his Jewish origin, yet in language felt himself a Greek. Thus he says (i. 424, quoted by Siegfried): ἔστι δὲ ὡς μὲν Ἑβραῖοι λέγουσι φανουὴλ ὡς δὲ ἡμεῖς ἀποστροφὴ θεοῦ.

While Plato is the author on whom he moulds his vocabulary, Philo proves himself in the direct line of the "Common" tradition by Aristotelian expressions like ἀΐδιος, ἀκροθώραξ, τονικός κ.τ.λ.; old Homeric words, such as ἀμενηνός, ἀνείμων, χανδόν κ.τ.λ., and poetical terms, of which ἄναγνος, ἀνακυκάω, and ἄτρυτος are examples. Still more, his vocabulary is in striking accord with that of Plutarch. It is needless to give instances from a common stock which comes up to many hundreds. Perhaps this may suggest that if we possessed remains as extensive of the other writers of the κοινή as those which are extant of Philo and Plutarch, we should find that the basis of vocabulary common to all of them was far wider and fuller than we are ready to suppose. Philo exemplifies very fully the characteristic of many words and expressions peculiar to himself, which has been so often referred to already. These are in great measure due to the " compounding " tendency of the post-Alexandrine Greek writers: *e.g.* δυσαιτιολόγητος, ἐξαδιαφορέω, ἐπεισφοιτάω, λογοϊατρεία, προεκτυπόω, τυφλοπλάστης, ψυχογόνιμος κ.τ.λ.

The special glossary for Philo is large and suggestive for the later language. He has a wonderful command of varied expression, and displays a strong tendency towards the use of synonyms. Thus pairs of words constantly appear in his writings: *e.g.* ἀκρατίζειν, ποτίζειν; γάνυσθαι, χαίρειν; ἐνδοιαστικός, διανοητικός; εὐθηνία, εὐετηρία; ὑπούλως, δολερῶς. He is fond of antitheses, and this probably accounts for much of his word-coining. So he opposes the αἰσχροπαθής to the αἰσχρουργός, διημερεύειν to διανυκτερεύειν, ἰδιῶται to ἐμπειροπόλεμοι, ἄνεσις to τόνωσις. Finally, like his contemporaries who have a mastery of the language, he delights in playing on words, as between κόρη, girl; κόρη, pupil of the eyes, and κατακορής, satiated.[1]

[1] The instances quoted are taken from the lists in Siegfried's *Philo*, pp. 32–136.

Josephus.—Following the succession chronologically, the next important name we meet is that of Josephus, who, like Philo, deserves special notice in connection with our investigation, as being, on the one hand, a Jew of Jerusalem, while, on the other, a man of thorough Greek cultivation. It will not be necessary, however, to say much on his vocabulary, as many of its characteristics have come up already in connection with other authors. His stock of words is very markedly that of the "Common" dialect. Perhaps, however, he is more persistent than any of the writers of the κοινή in his use of words which go back a long way in the history of Greek literature. A considerable percentage of his vocabulary is to be found in Herodotus, the Tragedians, and Xenophon. But a prominent element in his language is its striking agreement with that of Thucydides, whom he evidently made a chief model. This is emphasised by the fact that he follows Thucydides in the use of rare words and rare significations of words. To give one or two instances (all from a few chapters of the *Jewish Antiquities*)—

ἀξίωσις, ἀνοιμώττω, καλώδιον, ξύλωσις, περιαλγέω, προλοχίζομαι.

ἔδαφος in the phrase καθαιρεῖν εἰς τὸ ἔδαφος = raze to the ground = κατασκάπτειν εἰς ἔδαφος in Josephus. ἐγκεῖμαι = urge, entreat. ἐπικλάω = "bend" in sense of "turn to pity." ἄληπτος = hard to catch, etc. etc.

He appears to have less resemblance to Polybius in vocabulary than to any of the other authors of that whole period, while his affinity with Plutarch is most strongly marked. Only, in this connection very often the agreement is found where Plutarch himself uses words which belong to the older Ionic writers and the poetry of the language; and it is also worth noting that there is a considerable vocabulary common to Aristotle, Plutarch, and Josephus. Plato, too, supplies him with some rare words. There are few traces of "Hellenistic" to be discovered in his writing.

What renders Philo and Josephus of special moment for our inquiry is the fact that both of them make habitual use of the Septuagint version, and prize it greatly. Yet, though they are so thoroughly acquainted with this stereotyped "Hellenistic," which had become a standard for Jewish Greek, the power of real Greek influence with them is so strong as entirely, one may say, to repress any effect which the language of their sacred books might have upon their own vocabulary.

Plutarch.—This brings us to the last of the writers whom it is necessary to notice,—the Boeotian Plutarch,— whose name has occurred repeatedly in the course of our inquiry. Perhaps what specially characterises the vocabulary of Plutarch, viewed generally, is a sort of artificial picturesqueness, a more or less warm and vivid colouring, which does not, however, give the impression of spontaneity, but rather of a straining after artistic effect. His store of words is an enormous one, and it would be difficult to say with what authors he has most in common. Plato, at anyrate, would be one of these, and perhaps this may be to some extent accounted for by the fascination of that rich, artistic glow which his language exhibits. Plutarch, however, is a real and typical representative of the κοινή, and manifests all the characteristics which distinguish the "dialect." Accordingly he shows many affinities with Polybius, Diodorus, Philo, and the later writers. We have collected a list of fifty rare words which are common to Plutarch, Philo, and the New Testament. But when we recollect that the Lexicon for Plutarch is exceedingly comprehensive owing to the varied nature of his writings, it is natural that he should display, in a specially marked degree, characteristics which really belong to the whole range of the literary language.

To give some particulars[1]—

(1) There are the usual traces of Ionic influence seen in, e.g., the use of ἀπείπασθαι (mid.) = renounce, ἀτρεμεῖν, ἐξημεροῦν, σκορπίζεσθαι, φυγαδικῶς, etc.

(2) An exceptionally large number of non-classical words, including innumerable compounds: e.g. ἀντεξετάζεσθαι, διαμφισβήτησις, ἐγκαταστοιχειόω, ἐπιδιέξειμι (= recount), ἐκβαρβάρωσις, μισοπονηρία, προσεισπράττω, προσεξικμάζω, συνδιημέρευσις, φιλακόλαστος.

(3) Many poetical terms: e.g. ἄθραυστος, βιοτεύειν, ζόφος, κλυδών, πολύπονος, σέλας, etc.

(4) Numerous words in non-classical senses: ἀλύειν = loiter; ἄσπονδος = implacable; ἐπιεικῶς = usually; καταστρέφειν = turn upside down; παραγωγή = imposture; στεφανοῦν = reward; ὠφέλεια = booty.

Of course these last instances are not peculiar to Plutarch. Perhaps no writer of the κοινή, except Philo, is fitted to shed so much light on the language of the New Testament, and this fact is connected with a certain higher tone of diction in the New Testament writings

[1] Many of the examples are taken from Holden's most valuable editions of several of Plutarch's *Lives*.

which constantly elevates them above mere colloquialism, and so above the monotonous level of the Septuagint.

After this brief survey of the facts in the history of the Greek *literary* vocabulary, from Polybius to Plutarch, it may be well, in a sentence, to summarise our results.

It seems to us impossible to speak of a development, in the strict sense, being found, either in a downward or upward direction, in the language employed by the leading writers from the time of the LXX. to that of the New Testament. What we do meet with is rather a more or less stable basis of words which supports, so to speak, a constantly shifting surface. In other words, the earlier literary tradition, modified by the mixture of dialects and the weakened sense for language, has fixed, though not within rigid limits, a type of language distinct from the current popular speech, which becomes the standard for literature. This vocabulary is diversified by individual writers through personal predilections, local peculiarities, and the particular bias given by their own cast of thought.

CHAPTER VI

THE VOCABULARY OF THE NEW TESTAMENT

OUR historical sketch has now brought us to the vocabulary of the New Testament writings. Here we have to do with a sphere which is comparatively restricted, and so assertions can be made of a far more sweeping and positive kind than was possible in the case of the LXX. All the facts presented by the New Testament books are already within the range of investigation. But numerous problems, for whose solution data scarcely exist, come up as *à priori* questions in connection with the vocabulary of the New Testament. No doubt critics of all schools, or at least those free from violent prejudices, agree in fixing the limits of the New Testament books between 50 and 110 A.D. This is so far helpful. But very little fresh light is being gained as to the conditions and circumstances of the actual writers of the books. Even in the case of an author whose works are so well authenticated as those of St. Paul, all we know is that he used an amanuensis whose name is once given. In all probability this person, and any others who performed the same office, adhered strictly to the dictation of the apostle, but we cannot tell what special colouring may not have been thus introduced.

St. Peter also appears to have employed a secretary; and this must be connected with a variety of language, and a certain classical tone found in his writing.

The problem becomes still more complicated when we examine the Synoptic Gospels. Certainly it is becoming more and more one of the assured results of criticism that these have as their basis one common source, but it is hard to say whether this was Aramaic or Greek. Again, it is certain that "Matthew" and "Luke," as we have them, were compiled from other documents in addition to the "common source," and that some of these documents were known only to St. Luke. We cannot say in what language these additional sources were composed. Once more, the Gospels, or at least the first two, as we have them, may be redactions of the original documents, and so room may be left for one or more "hands" in the process, though it must be said that the arguments adduced on this point do not possess much force. These remarks show that we gain rather than lose by examining the New Testament vocabulary as a whole, and not in individual writers. For in any case the books of the New Testament, taken together as a single body of literature, display one particular type of writing, perhaps more varied in individual instances than is ever the case with the literary basis of the κοινή writers, yet marked off from all other Greek books by tendencies and modifications which are specially their own.

A careful calculation shows that the total number of words in the New Testament, excluding all proper names and their derivatives, is 4829. This contains the following separate elements:—

There are about 300 words from later Greek [1] in the N.T.
,, ,, 36 ,, ,, Hebrew ,, ,,
,, ,, 24 ,, ,, Latin ,, ,,
,, ,, 2 ,, ,, Foreign languages ,,
,, ,, 580 Biblical words, *i.e.* words only found in the LXX. and N.T.

Altogether, therefore, there are about 950 post-Aristotelian words, which, subtracted from the total number, 4829, leaves (roughly speaking) about 3850 in the New Testament which are found previous to the death of Aristotle, or about 80 per cent. of the whole vocabulary. These last figures are significant as showing an almost unexpected purity in the language of the New Testament viewed as a whole. It must, however, be noted that a large number of words, thoroughly current in good classical writers, receive, when employed in the New Testament, an entirely new sense.

As we have seen, there are, roughly speaking, about 950 post-Aristotelian words in the New Testament, *i.e.* about 20 per cent. of the whole vocabulary.

About 314 of these occur in the LXX., *i.e.* 33 per cent.
,, 104 ,, ,, Plutarch,[2] *i.e.* 10 ,,
,, 115 ,, ,, Polybius,[3] *i.e.* 11 ,,
,, 98 ,, ,, Philo,[4] *i.e.* about 10 ,,

Taking these general results, we are not justified in

---

[1] Post-Aristotelian secular Greek.
[2] *I.e.* not elsewhere before Plutarch.
[3] Not elsewhere before Polybius.
[4] Not elsewhere before Plato.

pronouncing the language of the New Testament to be a "vulgar" language. Yet one must not be misled by the statistics. The list of pre-Aristotelian words includes the prepositions, conjunctions, particles, and common adverbs, which are, of course, to be found in every Greek writer whose works are extant. The post-Aristotelian words, on the other hand, are almost exclusively nouns, verbs, and adjectives. But this rough and cursory glance at the constituent elements of the New Testament vocabulary may suffice to show that one is dealing here with a language which can be termed, at least in the broad sense, cultivated, and which comes unquestionably nearer the literary dialect of the period than does the language of the LXX.

Perhaps at this point, before we look at the vocabulary of the New Testament in its various relations, it may be well, as in the case of the LXX., to note down the results of an analysis of one of the New Testament books. St. Paul's Second Epistle to the Corinthians has been taken entirely at random, but as a good average specimen of Hellenistic writing from the pen of one who is a thorough Jew in his conceptions and root-ideas, and at the same time has had an exceptional amount of intercourse with the Gentile world lying around the Mediterranean.

Ordinary words have been omitted.

13 Chapters. 2 Corinthians. No. of Words examined = 164.

Of these 81 occur in the Septuagint.
,, 51 ,, ,, Plutarch.
,, 28 ,, ,, Polybius.
,, 27 ,, ,, Diodorus.
,, 27 ,, ,, Tragedians.

Of these 26 occur in Plato.
," 25 ," ," Josephus.
," 24 ," ," Aristotle.
," 22 ," ," Xenophon.
," 19 ," ," Philo.
," 18 ," ," Lucian.
," 15 ," ," Dionys. Hal.
," 13 ," ," Herodotus.
," 12 ," ," Hippocrates.
," 18 are peculiar to the N.T.

To bring out the general character of the New Testament vocabulary more clearly, the comparative table below is useful. A comparison of the vocabulary of Deuteronomy with that of 2 Corinthians gives something like the following proportion:—

Author.	Date.	New Testament.	Septuagint.
		Per cent.	Per cent.
Hippocrates	B.C. 430	8	10
Herodotus	,, 408	8	12
Tragedians	,, 470–406	17	14
Plato	,, 347	17	5
Aristotle	,, 322	14	...
Xenophon	,, 401	13	13
Polybius	,, 122	17	13
Diodorus	,, 40	17	7
Philo	A.D. 39	11	6
Josephus	,, 75	16	...
Plutarch	,, 120	31	16
Septuagint	B.C. (?) 280–130	37	12 % peculiar to itself
New Testament	A.D. 50–100	11 % peculiar to itself	50

It need hardly be said that these results are only

provisional. For the well-known authors they are probably fairly correct. But in the case of Philo, Diodorus, and Josephus, whose language has not been so thoroughly investigated, they must be regarded as approximately true. For our purpose, however, which is quite general in the present instance, they are valid.

(1.) One important general result is immediately obvious, which has been already hinted at. The New Testament vocabulary, as compared with the LXX., shows a far more distinct classical strain. This is exemplified in the table by the fact that in 2 Corinthians, 17 per cent. of the vocabulary is found in Plato, while 5 per cent. represents that author's share in the language of Deuteronomy. We are certain that less Hellenistic books of the New Testament, such as 1 Peter, Hebrews, and James, would show an even greater preponderance. This pure element is constantly showing itself. In parts of Hebrews and Acts one can sometimes forget for a moment that the Greek is Hellenistic. But the classical element in the New Testament vocabulary is usually made indistinct by the thoroughly Hellenistic character of the grammar and syntax. This is further helped by the Jewish cast of thought which underlies the actual words. Accordingly, in a book like the Epistle of St. James, where the Greek is forcible, and often beautiful, there always remains a certain Hellenistic monotony, a lack of flexibility, which mars the general impression.

In this connection there are many anomalies displayed by the various writers, difficult of explanation. Thus St. Matthew's Gospel, which has probably the most Hellenistic and Hebraistic tone of any New Testament book, and the least pretence to style, has fewer actual Hebraisms than the Gospel of St. Luke, and a far more even and natural flow than St. Mark's work, which is often rugged and inelegant. On the other hand, St. Luke, while capable of perhaps the most truly classical cast of language, goes beyond all the other New Testament writers in the use of vernacular expressions. No doubt these points have, underneath them, explanatory facts which have never come to light. But the minutiæ of individual variations only serve to give greater weight to phenomena of general agreement. Mistakes are often made by affixing the stamp of universal validity to what are only the predilections of individuals. Speaking generally, one may say that the desire after clearness and lucidity, which excludes all other aims, combined with the circumstances of the writers, their Jewish modes of thought, and the decay of the classical speech, made it impossible for classical Greek to be a predominating factor in the language of the New Testament. Yet it can be said with accuracy that its claims are far more powerfully vindicated in the sphere of vocabulary than in any other. Dry statistics render this unassailable. It is unnecessary, after what has been done in the case of the Septuagint, to attempt an analysis of the more ancient portion of the New Testament vocabulary. The elements which compose it are the same, though they are present in a greatly intensified degree, and specially so as regards the more classical portion of them.

(2.) One might reasonably expect that writers who, while thoroughly Hellenistic in their language, and thoroughly Jewish in their manner of thinking, could at times show a certain literary vigour and cultivation of speech,—one might expect that these writers must unconsciously reveal many points of meeting with the more purely literary works of their own age and the ages preceding and following their own. It could not be otherwise. Unless the language used is a mere popular jargon, the uncouth dialect of the streets, presuming to be literary, it will, though quite unconscious of direct literary influences, employ words and expressions which belong in common to all who have received education. Accordingly we find numerous relations between the authors of the "Common Dialect" and the New Testament writers. These relations are not found so much to hold of special classes of words. They rather belong to the language as a whole, though perhaps they are most prominently seen in connection with new compounds and words formed in various ways from elements which already exist in the ancient tongue. The New Testament vocabulary is about equally related to the vocabularies of Polybius, Diodorus, Philo, and Josephus. It must be said, however, that the resemblance to Philo is more important, as it is repeatedly found in the case of words which appear nowhere else in literature. There are fully twenty-five of these words, including terms so important as ἀπαύγασμα, ἀρχάγγελος, δίψυχος, κατηχέω, μετριοπαθέω, παλιγγενεσία, τετράδιον, ὑπόγραμμος, φιλαδελφία, χάρισμα.

Light will be thrown on the general character of the relation borne by the New Testament vocabulary to that of the κοινή writers by our giving a short table of rarer words common to Philo, the New Testament, and Plutarch :—

(ἄγρυπνος),[1] ἀκατάσχετος, ἀκυρόω, ἁλιεύω, ἅλυσις, ἀπελεύθερος, (ἀστείζομαι).
βόρβορος.
διανυκτερεύω, διάστημα.
ἐμπεριπατέω, ἐντρέφομαι, (ἐπακολούθημα), ἐπανόρθωσις, ἐπιορκέω, ἔσοπτρον, (εὐτονέω).
θανάσιμος, (θυρωρέω).
κατοπτρίζομαι, κατόρθωμα, κενοδοξία.
μεγαλαυχέω, μεγαλεῖον, (μεμψιμοιρέω), μετασχηματίζω, μετεωρίζω, (μετριοπάθεια), (μύωψ).
(νεωκορία), (νομοθέτημα), νοσφισμός.
(οἰκουρία), οἰνοφλυγία, (ὁμοφροσύνη).
παρακούω, (παραφροσύνη), παρεισέρχομαι, (παρεπιδημέω), παρηγορία, πειθαρχέω, περιλάμπω, περιπείρω, πλημμύρα, πολίτευμα, προετοιμάζω, προθεσμία, προϋπάρχω.
(ῥᾳδιουργός).
σαλεύω, (σκυθρωπάζω), συγκαταβαίνω, συγκρύπτω, συνεπιμαρτυρέω, συνθλίβω.
(φιλοφροσύνη).
χρηματίζω.
ψευδολογία.

Perhaps Plutarch stands nearest of all to the New Testament vocabulary, though this comes out especially in the case of certain books. In 2 Corinthians, as has been noted, 31 per cent. of the words occur in him as well. In the more narrative parts of the New Testament the proportion would be certainly far smaller. A good many of the coincidences in words are due, no doubt, to the subject-matter of Plutarch's works, and to their semi-philosophical colouring, which finds a parallel in the theological portions of the New Testament. But it

[1] The placing of a word within brackets means either that a derivative of it or the word from which it is derived occurs in the New Testament.

often happens that, besides the resemblances in vocabulary, Plutarch's use of words already found in classical authors sheds striking light on their significations in the New Testament.

(3.) The remarks made up to this point have only dealt with one side of the New Testament language, what may be termed the "literary" side. The point we have wished to emphasise is that the vocabulary of this collection of books cannot, with accuracy, be denominated "vulgar," seeing it possesses so many elements in common with the rest of Greek literature, four-fifths of it being pre-Aristotelian, and a considerable part of the remaining fifth belonging to the literary dialect of the time. These characteristics give it a distinct tone, which marks it as the property of educated men. They elevate it above the usual average of the Septuagint.

On the other hand, there remains a most important element of the New Testament vocabulary to be taken into account, that, in short, which, in addition to its Hebraistic colouring, marks it off as distinct both from the classical language of the great masters and the "Common" dialect of its literary contemporaries. We mean its "Colloquialism." This also is an element which might be looked for in the language of the New Testament. Its writers, almost without exception, were Jews. Most scholars agree that the vernacular of Palestine, strictly so called, was Aramaic. Greek was current in the country, in some parts more extensively than in others. It would naturally be the language of trade. The very fact that Greek would, in the first place, be acquired by the New Testament writers, entirely severed from Greek education and the influences of Greek culture, must inevitably give to it, on their lips, a particular stamp, and this could only be the colloquial tone which was familiar to them. After they had known the language for some time, and had settled in some particular district, for example, their vocabulary would or might assume a well-marked colouring, but the original colloquial basis would always remain. An additional reason for this was that they intended their writings to be, in the strictest sense, popular. That was their one aim. They did not appeal to a cultivated circle or to a literary audience. Their public consisted of freedmen, half-educated Asiatics, slaves, poor women, and the like. Thus the essential thing for them was to be intelligible. No writing could be too simple for the readers whom they addressed. But further, the great bulk of the persons for whom they wrote were either Jews of the Diaspora, or the mixed populations dwelling in the great centres of the new kingdoms which arose at the death of Alexander. This of itself determined their dialect. But the same public with whom they had to reckon, or, at least, one exactly similar, had, long before, come into possession of a body of literature written by Jews like themselves, and written in the Greek language. The translation of the Old Testament into Greek was an existing fact which proved the possibility of writing for the common people in a speech which they could easily understand. The language used then had been thoroughly vernacular. But Jews had now a more complete mastery of the Greek tongue. A kind of general culture had diffused itself everywhere, and even men of a foreign nation could not be insensible to it. Besides, the New Testament was not mere hack-work, so to speak. It was the free production of active minds thoroughly absorbed in their subject. This gave them a sort of natural eloquence, which had its effect on their language as well as on their style and tone. Still, their diction was thoroughly popular in character, essentially a *spoken* language, and not that of books, but yet the language spoken by men of education. This last fact makes it impossible to draw a hard and fast line round the New Testament vocabulary. Nowhere does an immovable barrier stand between it and the "Common" dialect.

The distinguishing feature, then, about the New Testament language is that it has for its regulating factor that type of colloquial Greek which originally prevailed in Egypt, which received a fixed form, or at least a standard, in the translation of the Old Testament, and which henceforward served as a linguistic basis for all Greek-speaking Jews. Some of the vernacular features which appear in the New Testament vocabulary have been treated in connection with the LXX., notably the constant employment of diminutives, well exemplified by St. Mark, who uses θυγάτριον, ἰχθύδιον, κοράσιον (several times), κυνάριον, παιδίον (several times), ὠτάριον. The instances of vernacular words, already given from the LXX., occur also in the New Testament.

But there is a further line of inquiry of great importance, which shows not only that the New Testament language contains a very large colloquial element, but that much of this element is no recent growth; that it has descended from an early period in the current popular speech of daily intercourse. We devote a good deal of space to it, as it has often been overlooked.

The Comic poets supply a valuable group of instances of words which are, at least, exceedingly rare outside their pages, and often found nowhere else, but which appear in the New Testament. We have collected fairly complete lists of these, which we give in full—

Rare Words, apparently of a mainly colloquial character, common to the Comic Poets (excluding Aristophanes) and the New Testament

α. ἀγγαρεύω. Menand. ([1] M. C. F. 4. 201).
  αἰσθητήριον. Diph. (M. 4. 383), Machon (M. 4. 497).
  ἁλιεύω. Plato Com. Europ. 2.
  ἀμέριμνος. Plat. (2. 697), Philem. (4. 41), Menan. (4. 239).
  ἀνάπηρος. Herm. (2. 393), Myrt. (2. 419).
  ἀπάρτι = ἀπὸ τοῦ νῦν. Plat. Com. Soph. 10.
  ἀργυροκόπος. Phryn. (2. 582).
  ἀρνίον. Eubul. (3. 212, 268), Philippid. (4. 476).
  ἀρραβών. Menan. (4. 268, 283), Antiph. (3. 66).
  ἀφρίζω. Antiph. (3. 95), Alexid. (3. 435).
  ἄχυρον. Six instances in Meineke.
β. βαλάντιον. Telecl. (2. 371).
  βαπτίζω. Aristophont. (3. 363), Eubul. (3. 238).
  βασανισμός. Alexid. (3. 515).
  βόθυνος. Cratin. (2. 137).
  βουνός. Philem. ap. Phryn. 133.
  βραβεῖον. Menan. (4. 653).
  βρέχω = ὕειν. Telecl. (2. 376), etc. etc.
  βρώσιμος. Diph. (4. 380), Anon. (4. 613).

[1] The passages in Meineke's *Fragmenta Comicorum Græcorum* are quoted.

γ. γλωσσόκομον. Timocl. (3. 590), Apoll. Carys. (4. 444).
γογγυσμός. Anax. (3. 174).
γυναικάριον. Diocl. (2. 840).
δ. δαιμονίζομαι. Philem. (4. 62).
διαπρίομαι. Eubul. (3. 255).
δύσφημος (-μία). Men. (4. 272).
ε. ἐγκομβόομαι. Epicharm. 3; Apoll. Carys. (4. 440).
ἔκβασις. Men. (4. 268).
ἐκμάσσω. Cratin. (2. 165).
ἐκτενῶς. Machon, *ap. Athen.* 13. 579 E.
ἐντρυφάω. Men. (4. 231).
ἐξανατέλλω. Telecl. (2. 373).
ἐπακροάομαι. Plat. (2. 618).
ἐπενδύτης. Nicoch. (2. 843).
ἐπίβλημα. Nicostr. Klin. 1.
ἐπικάλυμμα. Men. (4. 94).
ἐπιλησμόνη. Cratin. (2. 223), Alexid. (3. 525).
ἐπιστάτης = διδάσκαλος (as so often in St. Luke). Antiph. *ap. Antiatticista*, 96. 12.
ἐρίφιον. Athenion (4..558).
ἐσχάτως (ἔχειν). Menand. *ap. Photius.*
εὐαρεστέω. Lysipp. (2. 746).
εὐτόνως. Men. (4. 267).
εὐτραπελία. Posidipp. (4. 524).
εὐχαριστία. Men. (4. 267).
ἐφάπαξ. Eupolis (2. 498).
η. ἡμιώριον. Men. (4. 314).
θ. θερισμός. Eup. (2. 504).
θριαμβεύω, θρίαμβος. Cratin. (2. 36).
θυγάτριον. Xenarch. (3. 624), Men. (4. 198), Stratt. (2. 788), etc. etc.
ι. ἰχθύδιον. Eight different writers in Meineke.
κ. καμμύειν. Alexid. (3. 525).
κεραμικός. Sannyr. (2. 874).
κεράμιον. Alexid. (3. 409), Eubul. (3. 265), etc. etc.
κηπουρός. Archip. (2. 727), etc. etc.
κολλυβιστής. Menand. *ap. Phryn.* 404.
κολυμβάω. (Plato.) Pherec. (2. 300), Alexid. (3. 516).

κολυμβήθρα. (Plato.) Alexid. (3. 516).
κοπετός. Eup. (2. 492).
κοπρία. Stratt. (2. 779).
κοράσιον. Philippid. (4. 477).
κόφινος. Plat. (2. 629), Stratt. (2. 768), etc. etc.
κράββατος. Crito (4. 537).
κραιπάλη. Nicoch. (2. 846), Antiph. (3. 101), etc.
κυλίω. Anon. (4. 618).
κύμινον. Antiph. (3. 78), Alexid. (3. 437), Sotad. (3. 585).
κυρία. Philem. (4. 65).
λ. λάχανον. Nineteen instances in Meineke.
ληνός (?). Pherec. (2. 260), Men. (4. 104).
λιθάζω. Anaxand. (3. 169).
λίτρα. Posidipp. (4. 516), Diph. (4. 409).
μ. μακροθυμία. Men. (4. 238).
μάμμη. Pher. (2. 282).
μαστίζω (culinary sense). Eup. (2. 452), etc.
μεγιστᾶνες. Menand. ap. Phryn. 175.
μέθυσος. Menand. (4. 88).
μηλωτή. Philem. (4. 9).
μονόφθαλμος. Cratin. (2. 100).
μυκτηρίζω, μυκτηρισμός. Menand. (4. 314).
μυρίζω. Alcae. (2. 831), Antiph. (3. 81), etc.
μυστήριον = secret. Menander.
ν. νήθειν. Perh. Cratin. (2. 75), v.l. ἠθεῖν.
νωθρός. Amips. (2. 707), Anaxip. (4. 460).
ο. οἰνοφλυγία. Antiph. (3. 8).
ὀνάριον. Diph. (4. 417).
ὀπή. Sannyr. (2. 874), Xenarch. (3. 617).
ὀπήτιον. Nicoch. (2. 844).
ὅρασις. Men. (4. 105).
ὀστράκινος. Plat. (2. 654).
ὀψάριον. Fourteen instances in Meineke.
ὀψώνιον. Men. ap. Phryn. 393. Thugen. (4. 593).
π. παθητός. Men. Sentent. 457.
παιδάριον. Eleven instances in Meineke.
πανδοχ(-δοκ-)εῖον. Philippid. (4. 474).
παρεμβολή. Theoph. (3. 630), Crito (4. 537).

THE VOCABULARY OF THE NEW TESTAMENT 75

παροψίς. Antiph. ap. Athen. 9. 367 D.
πενιχρός. (Hom., Theogn., Pind.), Philetaer. (3. 293), Diod. (3. 544).
περιζώννυμι. Theoph. (2. 807), Anaxand. (3. 183).
πήγανον. Alexid. (3. 437).
πλοιάριον. Men. (4. 88).
πνικτός. Antiph. 'Αγροικ. 1. 4; Stratt. (2. 774), Alexid. (3. 439).
πολυποίκιλος. Eub. (3. 252).
πολύτιμος. Epicharm. ap. Athen. 7. 7; Men. (4. 101).
προβατικός. Eupol. (2. 427).
✓ προσκεφάλαιον = boat-cushion. Cratin. (2. 170), Herm. (2. 404).

ρ. ῥαβδίζω. Pherec. (2. 273).
ῥάπισμα. Antiph. (3. 126).
ῥαφίς. Epichar. (Bekk. Anecd. 113), Archip. ap. Poll. 10. 136.
ῥιπίζω. Antiph. (3. 117), Anon. 4. 615.
› ῥύμη. Antiph. (3. 26), Philippid. (4. 471).
ῥυπαρός. Telecl. (2. 364), Pherec. (2. 290), Eupol. (2. 557), etc.
ῥυπόω. Anaxand. (3. 177), Aristophont. (3. 362), etc.

σ. σανδάλιον. Cratin. (2. 91), Cephis. (2. 884), Theoph. (2. 809), etc.
σαπρός = filthy, αἰσχρός. Pherec. ap. Theon., prob. Philem. Incert. 47.
σαργάνη. Timocl. (3. 600).
σαρδόνυξ. Philem. (4. 66), Men. (4. 307).
σεμίδαλις. Herm. (2. 408), Stratt. (2. 764), etc.
σίναπι. Archip. ap. Ath. 9. 68; Anaxip. (4. 460).
σιτευτός. Epigen. (3. 537).
σκηνοποιός. Anon. (4. 680).
σπυρίς. Six instances in Meineke.
στάμνος. Chiefly Comic. Four instances in Meineke.
στιγμή. Men. (4. 312).
στρηνιᾶν. Antiph. ap. Ath. 3. 127. Sophil. ap. Ath. 3. 100.
στρῆνος. Nicostr. (5. 84).

στρουθίον. Anaxand (3. 164), Ephipp. (3. 326).
συκάμινος. Amphid. (3. 318).
συμμαθητής. Anaxipp. (4. 459).
συμπαθής. (Aristot.), Plato Com. (2. 686).
συνθλάω. Alexid. (3. 510).
συνοδία. Men. Sentent. 24.
σύρω. Anaxil. (3. 345), Eub. (3. 242).
σύσσημον. Men. ap. Phryn. 393.
σχοίνιον. Chiefly Comic. Four instances in Meineke.
σωρεύω { σώρευμα. Eub. (3. 228).
         { σωρευτός. Alexid. (3. 416).
τ. τελώνιον. Posidipp. (4. 517).
τρυγών. Six instances in Meineke.
τρύπημα. Eup. (2. 562). Vernacular word.
τρώγω. (Colloquial.) Sixteen instances in Meineke.
τυρβάζω. Alexid. (3. 395).
φ. φαιλόνης, φαινόλης. Rhinthon ap. Poll.
φανός. Six instances in Meineke.
φιλαδελφία. Alexid. (3. 526).
φλύαρος. Men. (4. 236).
φόρτιον. Eight instances in Meineke.
φύραμα. Mens. (3. 569).
χ. χαλκίον. Ten instances in Meineke.
χάρτης. Plato, Fragg. 10, p. 257.
χειραγωγός. Philem. (4. 47).
χλιαρός. Five instances in Meineke.
χορτάζω (of men). Eight instances in Meineke.
(χορτασμός. Anaxand. [3. 202].)
ω. ὠρύομαι. Plat. (2. 659).

We have given these lists very fully because we believe that no more important evidence could be presented with regard to the colloquial character of the New Testament vocabulary. In the Comic poets, if anywhere, we should expect to find the current popular speech strongly marked. And when words meet us all through the Comic literature of Greece, from Cratinus at its beginning to Posidippus at its close, which scarcely appear anywhere else except in the New Testament, we are justified in accepting this as proof positive of our position. The facts exhibited show clearly the existence of a language of popular intercourse from an early time, which verges on the borders of the literary language, but is excluded from composition except in the case of Comedy. Yet many of the words in question must have borne the stamp of refinement, and belonged to the diction of polite speech at a period long antecedent to literary production. By processes which can no more be discovered, these words have somehow lost caste, and while by no means rejected altogether, we may believe, from the conversation of the educated, have come to be regarded as more or less "vulgar" and "rough." In this way the door of literature was barred to them. But they continued all along to have full play in the language of daily life, and accordingly, when Greek literary taste began to decay, and the real literary dialect no longer survived in spontaneous form, these words again asserted themselves, and by the time the New Testament was written, they have regained their place in the language of educated men, and are found occasionally even in the writers of the "Common Dialect."

But in addition to the writers we have quoted, who range over a period of three hundred years, and whose works are only extant in a very fragmentary form, a most interesting and important contribution is made to the history of colloquial Greek in connection with the language of the New Testament by the vocabulary of Aristophanes. In his case we have the advantage of seeing the phenomena of the Greek popular vocabulary at a *definite stage* in Greek history. So a landmark is given by which the past of the colloquial language and its future may be estimated. Besides, Aristophanes lived in the Golden Age of the Attic dialect, when the sense for language had reached its highest pitch. Accordingly, one may expect that the "popular" words admitted by him are, at least, on the higher level of the "conversational" type of speech. This gives an additional criterion for the New Testament vocabulary. The following is a list of rare words which occur in Aristophanes, and almost nowhere else except in the New Testament. They are all apparently "colloquial":—

α. ἄβυσσος. Ran. 138.
ἄκρατον. Ach. 75, 1229; Eq. 85, 87.
ἀμπελουργός. Pax 190.
ἄμφοδον. Frag. 304.
ἀνθρακία. Eq. 780.
ἀπομάσσομαι. Eq. 819.
β. βάτος. Frag. 593.
βδελύσσομαι. Ten instances = loathe.
βιβλιδάριον (N.T. βιβλαρίδιον). Frag. (Mein. 2. 1207).
δ. διάλεκτος. Frag. 552.
ε. ἐκκολυμβάω. Frag. (2. 975).
ἐκπτύω. Vesp. 792.
ἐκστρέφω. Plut. 721; Nub. 88, 554.
ἐμβάπτω. Frag. 205; Nub. 150.
ἐμφυσάω. Vesp. 1219.
ἐννεύω. Frag. (2. 980).
ἐντυλίσσω. Plut. 692; Nub. 987.
εὐκόπως. Frag. 615.
εὐτόνως. Plut. 1095.
η. ἡδύοσμος. Frag. (2. 1178).

θ. θλίβω. Fig. sense in Vesp. 1289; Ran. 5. So θλίψις in N.T.
θυρίς. Vesp. 379; Therm. 797.
ι. ἱκανός. In vernac. sense of "long," "many"; Pax 354.
κ. κάρφος. Av. 643; Vesp. 249; Lys. 474.
κειρία. Av. 816.
κέρμα. Plut. 379; Av. 1108.
κλινίδιον. N.T. κλινάριον. Frag. 2. 1046.
κοιτών. Frag. (2. 947).
κόλλυβος. Pax 1200. A word of trade, said to be Phœnician; cf. N.T. κολλυβιστής.
κυλλός. Eq. 1083; Av. 1379.
λ. λαλιά. Nub. 931; Ran. 1069. With a notion of contempt.
λάρυγξ. Ran. 575; Eq. 1363.
μ. μασ(σ)άομαι. Six times in Aristoph.
μυκτῆρες = "critic nostrils." Ran. 893; cf. N.T. μυκτηρίζειν.
ν. νουθεσία. Ran. 1009.
νύττω. Nub. 321; frag. in Homer; prob. came to be colloquial.
ο. ὀθόνιον. Frag. (2. 989).
οἰνοποτίς (N.T. οἰνοπότης). Therm. 393.
ὄρθρος (βαθύς). Prob. vernac. expression; Vesp. 216.
π. παγίς. Av. 194, 527; Frag. 663.
παρακύπτω. Extremely freq. in Aristoph.
πρόδρομος. Metaph. in Aristoph. and Comic writers.
προσκυλίω. Vesp. 202.
πρότερον = superior. Ran. 76.
ρ. ῥαβδοῦχος. Pax 734.
σ. σάκκος. Ach. 745 (a Megarian is speaking, hence two κ's).
τ. τρίβολος. Lys. 576.
τρύβλιον. Ach. 278; Av. 77.
τυρβάζομαι. Pax 1007; Vesp. 257.
υ. ὑάλινος. Ach. 74.
ὑπάγω = go. Colloq. use; Ran. 174; Nub. 1298; Vesp. 290.

ὑπωπιάζω. Pax 541.
φ. φιμόω. Nub. 592.
ψ. ψωμίζω. Therm. 692; Lys. 19; Eq. 715.

Before leaving the Comic poets, it is worth our while to note that, even among the earlier ones, strange compounds and clumsy formations are found, which are exact prototypes of the same phenomena in the late Greek of post-Alexandrine days.

Thus Crates employs words like ἐθελόσυχνος, ἀναβιώσασθαι = ποιῆσαι ἀναβιῶσαι, etc.

Eupolis uses ἀμβλυστονῆσαι, ἀφαδία, βδελυρεύομαι, νεανισκέω, etc.

In Phrynichus occur such forms as συβαριασμός, τευτάζεσθαι ὑπερηλιάζομαι, etc.

αὐτοσχεδίασμα, ἐπινωτίζειν, κολλοπεύω, παντοπωλία, and the like, which occur in the old Comedy, look quite like formations belonging to the age of the LXX.

The old "Anonymous Writer" on Comedy expressly says that the poets of the Middle Comedy employed τῆς συνήθους λαλίας. By this time the inhabitants of Athens had come into frequent contact with foreigners and men who spoke impure Greek. This told on the language of the people, and, of course, reflected itself in the vocabulary of the Comic poets. By the time the New Comedy arose, the tendencies already in vogue had increased in influence. The one aim the poets set before them was that which we saw to be the chief thing also with Hellenistic writers, viz. clearness and intelligibility. And so *Anonymus de Com.* p. 32, says: ἡ μὲν νέα τὸ σαφέστερον ἔχει τῇ νέᾳ κεχρημένη Ἀτθίδι, ἡ δὲ παλαιὰ τὸ δεινὸν καὶ ὑψηλὸν τοῦ λέγειν. Barbarous words and forms received far greater licence, and this because "Comedy follows the common language of the people."

One point which bears upon the relation of the New Testament vocabulary to the spoken language remains to be glanced at. It is found that in the New Testament (and to a considerable extent in the Comic writers) words which in ordinary Greek bore a strong and almost coarse sense, have become entirely enervated, so that they are used in the most casual and trivial connections. This fact is easily explained. The terms gradually passed into the daily speech of the people, a process in which, quite naturally, the rough edges were worn off, and they became strictly commonplace words. Instances are the following:—

βάλλω. In the Class. language usu. = throw, hurl, cast. Looser sense in Homer and Tragedians, where it is often used metaphorically, but has a notion of "haste" or "hurry" associated with it. This use is almost always the equivalent of our "*lay* to heart."

In N.T. often = "*put*" in its most colourless sense.

E.g. Mark 7. 33: ἔβαλεν τοὺς δακτύλους εἰς τὰ ὦτα αὐτοῦ.

John 20. 27: φέρε τὴν χεῖρά σου καὶ βάλε εἰς τὴν πλευράν μου.

John 5. 7: ἵνα ὅταν ταραχθῇ τὸ ὕδωρ βάλῃ με εἰς τὴν κολυμβήθραν (used of a sick man).

ἐρεύγω, ἐρεύγομαι. In Class. Gk. (1) Disgorge, Hom.; (2) Surge, Hom. Pind.; (3) In one or two places in Homer = roar.

In N.T. Matt. 13. 35 (quotation fr. LXX.): ἀνοίξω

ἐν παραβολαῖς τὸ στόμα μου, ἐρεύξομαι κεκρυμμένα ἀπὸ καταβολῆς κόσμου = utter.

Cf. Theocr. 13. 58 : τρὶς μὲν Ὕλαν αὖσεν ὅσον βαθὺς ἤρυγε λαιμός. This sense is found several times in the LXX.

σκύλλω. In Aesch. and Anthol. = flay, mangle.

In N.T. = annoy. E.g. Mark 5. 35 : τί ἔτι σκύλλεις τὸν διδάσκαλον. So Matt. 10. 36 : ἐσκυλμένοι = worn out, worried. σκυλμός in LXX. (and Cicero's *Letters*) = troubles.

τρώγω. In Homer, used of animals = gnaw, munch, crunch.

In Hdt., etc., of men, but only of eating vegetables, fruit, etc. Through vernacular usage it came to mean "eat" in general.

In N.T. always used in this sense. In the fourth Gospel it is employed to the complete exclusion of ἐσθίειν.

Cf. John 6. 54 : ὁ τρώγων μου τὴν σάρκα.

Matt. 24. 38 : τρώγοντες καὶ πίνοντες.

χορτάζειν, χορτάζομαι. In earlier Greek, uniformly of animals = feed, fatten with fodder. In Comedy, used of men feasting; and then, through colloquial Greek = "eat," with no strong sense attached. This softened use also in Comedy.

In N.T. used invariably = eat, or, satisfy with food.

All distinction between ἐσθίειν and χορτάζεσθαι has by this time vanished. An interesting illustration of this is Mark 7. 27, 28 : ἄφες πρῶτον χορτασθῆναι τὰ τέκνα· . . . τὰ κυνάρια ὑποκάτω τῆς τραπέζης ἐσθίουσιν ἀπὸ τῶν ψιχίων τῶν παιδίων. Same use in LXX.

Words which have passed through the same process are—

κραυγάζειν	used as	= καλεῖν.
πιέζειν (πιάζειν)	,,	= ἅπτεσθαι.
ψηλαφᾶν	,,	= investigate, etc.

They are all, apparently, colloquial usages, whose process of formation has been accelerated by the tendency to exaggerate which a language shows when it has entered on a period of degeneration.

One most important element in the New Testament vocabulary we merely mention here as it must come up for elaborate treatment afterwards, viz. the large number of terms belonging to the sphere of Christian Theology which occur throughout these writings.

CHAPTER VII

COMPARISON OF THE VOCABULARY OF THE SEPTUAGINT WITH THAT OF THE NEW TESTAMENT

WE have attempted in the foregoing pages to lay a more or less solid basis for our investigation, to indicate the directions in which it must proceed and its limits, and to accumulate various lines of evidence which must have a chief place in determining its issue. We have tried to sketch the special conditions of the Greek language in the age when the LXX. arose. A rough analysis of the main elements in the vocabulary of the LXX. has been given, and it has been endeavoured to connect this discussion with a similar examination of the New Testament language by means of a very brief inquiry into the vocabulary of the Common Dialect. A survey of the New Testament vocabulary has completed the collection of materials necessary both for placing us at the proper point of view for our discussion, and for supplying us with guiding-lines throughout the whole of the investigation.

What remains to be done in the second part of this dissertation is to state generally the facts which come to view on a minute comparison of the vocabulary of the LXX. with that of the New Testament, to illustrate these, to draw the legitimate inferences from them, and so arrive at some definite conclusion with respect to the whole question under examination.

The most cursory reading of the Greek New Testament shows a constant habit on the part of the writers of quoting from the Old Testament. The significant fact in this connection is that the great majority of these quotations are from the Greek version of the Sacred Books. When it is remembered that the writers are almost all Jews, and that the Jewish reverence for the actual letters of the Hebrew original of the Old Testament is unparalleled, the point attracts attention. Unfortunately it is exceedingly difficult to discover the actual usage of the Palestinian synagogues with respect to the reading of the Old Testament in the first century A.D. Some scholars assert that the synagogue readers must have employed Targums in Aramaic, the vernacular of the country. Others as boldly declare that it was the Greek version and no other which was read in the public services. And this is used as an argument in favour of the position, that Greek, equally with or more than Aramaic, was the popular language of the country in the time of Christ.

Without, however, discussing a question which seems impossible of solution, one may with safety affirm that the LXX. must have been well known at least to the great mass of intelligent and educated Jews, for this is a legitimate inference from the New Testament. There we find that there are about three hundred quotations from the Old Testament. At least ninety of these agree verbally with the LXX. In the others, the variations from it are very trifling. More important still, in thirty-seven of the ninety the LXX. differs from the Hebrew text. Accordingly, the writers of the New Testament must have been thoroughly acquainted with this version, seeing they preferred to use it, though written in a foreign language, rather than to translate from a text which they regarded as in the strictest sense inspired. No doubt it must be borne in mind that the readers for whom they wrote were chiefly "Gentiles," to whom the Old Testament would only be known in its Greek dress. Still their easy familiarity with it shows how completely they had made it their own. This is corroborated by constant reminiscences of it, and allusions which are almost more important than quotations in this connection, as coming up unconsciously. And so the question naturally arises: If these writers were so thoroughly versed in the Greek translation of the Old Testament, as is certainly the fact, is it not likely that when they came to write books in Greek themselves, their language would be moulded and shaped by the language of the LXX., especially as the latter had stereotyped a particular form of Greek, and had so become a standard for Hellenistic Jews? Is it not likely that the influence of the LXX. will appear, not only in words which express Hebrew conceptions and feelings, but in the general vocabulary which the Jewish writers of the New Testament employ?

A scholar so thorough and so original as the late Dr. Hatch says, in his *Essays in Biblical Greek* (p. 34): "The great majority of New Testament words are words which, though for the most part common to biblical and contemporary secular Greek, express in their biblical use the conceptions of a Semitic race, and which must consequently be examined by the light of the cognate documents which form the LXX." And again (p. 11): "Biblical Greek is thus a language which stands by itself. What we have to find out in studying it is what meaning certain Greek words conveyed to a Semitic mind." Our attempt in the pages that follow must be to test these statements by means of the facts we have to produce, and in the light of the conclusions arrived at in the former part of the dissertation.

There are various ways in which the vocabulary of one group of writings may be presumed to be a principal factor in the formation of that which belongs to another group. There must always be more or less of mere presumption about the matter, because the life-history of words is often silent and curious. Let us call the earlier group A, and the later B.

(1.) There is, first, what may be called external evidence. We may have a definite knowledge of the fact that the writers of B were intimately acquainted with group A, that, indeed, this was almost their only literature. So a presumption is legitimate that the language of A will influence in an indefinite degree the language of B. But this is purely *à priori*.

(2.) On examination, it may be found that an overwhelmingly large proportion of the vocabulary of B has already occurred in A. This leads us to look for further points of resemblance.

(3.) A careful scrutiny of the two vocabularies may show that a large number of words found in B occur in no other known writings except group A.

(4.) It may appear that many of the words common to A and B are derived words, whose special character makes it certain that they were formed by the writers of A.

(5.) We may further discover that a large number of current words, found in other authors, occur in A and B in a sense quite peculiar to these two groups of writings.

(6.) A set of words may be found in B which are local peculiarities of the region where group A arose.

This rough classification probably embraces most of the relations which could exist between two vocabularies. Bearing them in mind, we must set down the facts which emerge on a comparison of the vocabulary of the LXX. with that of the New Testament.

We have already seen that out of a total vocabulary of over 4800 words in the New Testament (excluding all proper names and their derivatives) there are about 950 which are post-Aristotelian; of these, over 300 are found also in the LXX. But one half of this number occurs in other writings, which, in this case, mean those of the "Common Dialect," the Anthology, the Jewish Apocrypha, Philo, and Inscriptions. On this element, it is plain, no valid conclusions can be based, except that special attention must be directed to the group common to the LXX., the New Testament, and Philo. We shall touch on this immediately. There are, then, about 150 words in all which are strictly peculiar to the LXX. and New Testament. The following is a list which we have compiled of them. It is, at least, approximately correct:—

Nouns—
ἀγαθωσύνη, ἀγαλλίασις, ἁγιασμός, ἁγιωσύνη, αἴνεσις, ἀλίσγημα, ἀνταπόδομα, ἀποκάλυψις.

βάτος, βδέλυγμα, βροχή.
γέεννα, γνώστης, γυμνότης.
δότης.
ἐλεγμός, ἔλεγξις, ἐμπαιγμός, ἐμπαίκτης, ἔνταλμα, ἐπισκοπή, ἐρήμωσις, εὐδοκία, ἐφημερία.
ἥττημα.
θέλησις.
ἱεράτευμα.
καθαρισμός, κατάνυξις, κατοικητήριον, καύσων, καύχησις, κόρος.
λύτρωσις.
ματαιότης, μεγαλειότης, μεγαλωσύνη, μετοικέω, μοιχαλίς.
νῖκος.
ὁλοκληρία, ὀπτασία, ὁρκωμοσία.
παραπικρασμός, παροικία, παροργισμός, πατριάρχης, πειρασμός, περικάθαρμα, περισσεία, πρόσκομμα.
ῥαντισμός.
σαβαώθ, σαγήνη, σατανᾶς, σάτον, σίκερα, σκάνδαλον, σκληροκαρδία.
ὑπακοή, ὑπάντησις, ὑπολήνιον, ὑστέρημα.
φώστηρ.
ψιθυρισμός.
ὠτίον.

Adjectives—
ἀκρογωνιαῖος, ἀλλογενής, ἀμέθυστος, ἀνεξιχνίαστος, ἀνθρωπαρεσκός.
δεκτός.
λαξευτός, λειτουργικός.
μίσθιος, μογίλαλος.
ὀλιγόψυχος.
περιούσιος, πρωϊνός.
σητόβρωτος, σκληροτράχηλος.
ταπεινόφρων.

Verbs—
ἀγαθοποιέω, ἀγαλλιάω, ἁγιάζω, αἰχμαλωτεύω, ἀμφιάζω, ἀναζώννυμι, ἀναθεματίζω, ἀποδεκατεύω, ἀποκεφαλίζω, ἀποφθέγγομαι.

βεβηλόω.
γογγύζω.
δεκατόω, διαγογγύζω, δολιόω, δυναμόω.
εἰρηνοποιέω, ἐκζητέω, ἐκμυκτηρίζω, ἐκπειράζω, ἐκπορνεύω, (ἐκριζόω), ἐνδιδύσκω, ἐνδοξάζω, ἐνδυναμόω, ἐνευλογέω, ἐνκαινίζω, ἐνταφιάζω, ἐνωτίζομαι, ἐξαστράπτω, ἐξολεθρεύω, ἐξουδενέω, ἐξυπνίζω, ἐπαναπαύω, ἐπιγαμβρεύω, ἐπιφαύσκω. (ἱερατεύω.)
καθαρίζω, κατακαυχάομαι, κατακληρονομέω, κατανύσσω, κλυδωνίζομαι, κραταιόω.
μακροθυμέω, ματαιόω.
ὀλοθρεύω, ὀρθοτομέω, ὀπτάνω, ὀρθρίζω.
παγιδεύω, παραζηλόω, πληροφορέω, προσοχθίζω.
ῥαντίζω.
στυγνάζω, στήκω, συνεγείρω.
ὑπερυψόω.

Adverbs—
ἑβδομηκοντάκις, ἔναντι, ἐνώπιον, ἐξαίπνα, ἐπαύριον. κατενώπιον.

Interjections—
ἀμήν, ἀλληλούια.
οὐαί.

We add as an appendix to this list those words which are common to the LXX., New Testament, and Philo. (This list is probably not so complete as the former.)

Nouns—
ἀγάπη, ἀκροβυστία, ἀπαύγασμα.
διασπορά, διαταγή, δίδραχμον.
ἐνκαίνια.
θυσιαστήριον.
ἱλασμός.
καταπέτασμα, κατάσχεσις, καταφρονητής, κόκκινος.
λυτρωτής.
μάννα.

ὁλοκαύτωμα.
παντοκράτωρ, πάσχα, πεποίθησις, προσευχή, προσήλυτος, προφητεία, πρωτοτοκία.
σάββατον.
ὕσσωπος, ὕψωμα.
φωτισμός.
χερουβείν.
ψευδοπροφήτης.

Adjectives—
ἀπερίτμητος.
βδελυκτός.
δυσβάστακτος.
ἐπικατάρατος, εὐλογητός.
ἱλαστήριος.
πρωτότοκος.

Verbs—
ἀνταποκρίνομαι.
ἐκπειράζω, ἐμπεριπατέω, ἐξομολογέω.
παραπικραίνω.

The lists just given show the *nature* of the relation which can be proved by actual facts to exist between the vocabularies of the LXX. and New Testament. We have included the words common to these with Philo, because (1) Philo was a Jewish writer. (2) He lived in Alexandria, the home of the LXX. (3) All through his works he shows a remarkable acquaintance with the LXX., which is usually the text on which he comments. Accordingly, when we find him using a set of terms of a peculiar character,—as a rule, tinged with an Old Testament colouring,—there is, to say the least, a very strong presumption that he derived them from the LXX.

But before leaving our dry columns of statistics, which

must form the basis of all that has yet to be done, one list more needs to be presented. There is a considerable number of words found in Greek writers of all periods, more or less, which appear in the New Testament in an altogether peculiar and abnormal sense. A large number of those are found in the LXX. either with an identical or closely-connected signification. It seems advisable to insert a list of these here, so as to avoid the necessity of interrupting our subsequent discussion. It must be noted that the great majority of them are found in the New Testament in their *ordinary* sense as well.

WORDS COMMON TO THE LXX. AND N.T. WITH "BIBLICAL" MEANING.

Nouns—
ἄγγελος, ἀδελφός, ἀντίληψις, ἀντιλογία, ἀποστάσιον.
γραμματεύς.
διάβολος (ὁ), δόξα, δῶμα, δωρεά.
ἔθνος, εἴδωλον, εἰρήνη, ἐκκλησία, ἔκστασις, ἐπισκοπή, εὐλογία.
ἡμέρα.
θάνατος, θεός, θυγάτηρ.
ἱλασμός, ἱλαστήριον.
κακία, καρπός, κατάπαυσις, κέρας, κήρυγμα, κληρονόμος, κοιλία, κοπή, κόσμος, κρίσις, κριτής.
λύτρωσις.
μακροθυμία, μοιχαλίς, μυστήριον.
νόμος, νύμφη.
ὄνομα, οὐρανός, ὀχύρωμα.
παιδεία, παῖς, παραβολή, πάροικος, πειρασμός, πορνεία, πρόσωπον, προφήτης.
ῥῆμα, ῥίζα.
σάρξ, σκάνδαλον, σκηνοπηγία, στόμα, στρατιά, σύντριμμα, σωτήρ, σωτηρία, σωτήριον.

[1] Based entirely on the excellent Lists in Thayer's edition of Grimm-Wilke's *Clavis Novi Testamenti*. T. & T. Clark.

τέκνον.
υἱός, ὑποκριτής.

Adjectives—
ἐκλεκτός, μωρός.

Verbs—
ἀδυνατέω, ἀναφέρω, ἀνθομολογέομαι, ἀποκαλύπτω, ἀποκρίνω, ἀφυστερέω, αὐγάζω.
διατίθεμαι, δικαιόω, δοξάζω.
εἴδω, εἰμί, εἶπον, ἐκλέγομαι, ἐξομολογέω, ἐπερωτάω, ἐπιγαμβρεύω, ἐπικαλέω, ἐπισκέπτομαι, ἐρεύγομαι, εὐδοκέω, εὐλογέω.
ζωογονέω.
ἡσυχάζω.
θέλω, θροέω.
ἰσχύω.
καθεύδω, κακόω, κακαλογέω, καμμύω, κάμπτω, καταισχύνω, κρίνω, κοπιάω.
λικμάω.
μακροθυμέω, μωραίνω.
παιδεύω, πατάσσω, πειράζω, πορεύω, προστίθημι, προφητεύω.
συνάγω, συντελέω, σώζω.
φυλάσσω, φωτίζω.

Our results may be briefly summarised thus—

(1.) There are, roughly speaking, about 550 words which may be termed "Biblical," *i.e.* found either in the New Testament alone, or, besides, only in the LXX. That is, about 12 per cent. of the total vocabulary of the New Testament is "Biblical."

(2.) About 30 per cent. of the total number of "Biblical" words in the New Testament occur in the LXX.

(3.) About 32 per cent. of the words found in the New Testament alone with special "Biblical" meaning occur in the LXX.

CHAPTER VIII

THE INFLUENCE OF THE SEPTUAGINT ON THE THEO-
LOGICAL AND RELIGIOUS TERMS OF THE NEW TESTA-
MENT VOCABULARY

WE have seen that the LXX. was thoroughly well-known to the writers of the New Testament. But these latter had a peculiar task before them. The main object of their writing was to set forth to Jews and Greeks alike the conceptions of that new Faith which had won their allegiance. These conceptions were, of course, religious and theological. The problem was to express them in a suitable terminology. But they had a model to follow. Already the religious and theological ideas of the Hebrew people had been clothed in a Greek dress. This had involved many difficulties, but they had been in great measure surmounted. So that there was a technical theological vocabulary actually existing. But Christian modes of thinking were a thorough advance on those of the Hebrews. Often, therefore, entirely new words had to come into use to express the new ideas, or else old words had to undergo a large extension of meaning. Still, the early Christian writers, being almost all Jews, retained a Hebrew colouring throughout their thought. There was a basis of Hebrew ideas beneath the new superstructure. Accordingly, even in the case of purely Christian conceptions, it was thoroughly natural for the New Testament writers to frame their language on the analogy of the existing theological vocabulary which they found in the Greek version of the Old Testament.

Considering these circumstances, then, we should expect to find the vocabulary of the LXX. exercising a direct influence on that of the New Testament in regard to religious and theological terms. Strangely enough, we discover that this particular class of terms does *not* include as a main element words either formed or brought into literature for the first time by the LXX. The most of them fall within that class of "Words common to the LXX. and New Testament with 'Biblical' signification," of which a list has already been given. Of course, a large number belong to the New Testament *alone*.

Here there can be no discussion. Facts clearly show how prominent a part the LXX. plays in moulding the *religious* vocabulary of the New Testament. As this is one of the most important phenomena in connection with the relation of the two vocabularies, it must be fully illustrated. And it is perhaps well, in estimating the influence of the LXX. on the language of the New Testament, to begin with a class of words where that influence is too obvious to be mistaken. Our examples are given simply in alphabetical order.

Nouns

ἀδελφός—
 I. In Class. Lit. in the ordinary sense.
 II. In LXX.—(1) = brother. (2) = neighbour. Lev. 19. 17:

οὐ μισήσεις τὸν ἀδελφόν σου τῇ διανοίᾳ σου· ἐλεγμῷ ἐλέγξεις τὸν πλησίον σου. (3) = member of the same nation, Ex. 2. 14: Μωυσῆς ἐξῆλθεν πρὸς τοὺς ἀδελφοὺς αὐτοῦ τοὺς υἱοὺς Ἰσραήλ; Deut. 15. 3: τὸν ἀλλότριον ἀπαιτήσεις ὅσα ἐὰν ᾖ σοι παρ' αὐτῷ, τοῦ ἀδελφοῦ σου ἄφεσιν ποιήσεις τοῦ χρέους σου.

III. In N.T.—(1) ordinary sense. (2) = neighbour, Matt. 7. 3: τὸ κάρφος τὸ ἐν τῷ ὀφθαλμῷ τοῦ ἀδελφοῦ σου. (3) = member of the same nation, Rom. 9. 3: ηὐχόμην γὰρ ἀνάθεμα εἶναι αὐτὸς ἐγὼ ἀπὸ τοῦ Χριστοῦ ὑπὲρ τῶν ἀδελφῶν μου, τῶν συγγενῶν μου κατὰ σάρκα οἵτινές εἰσιν Ἰσραηλεῖται. (4) = fellow-Christians, the whole band of Christians being looked on as forming a single family, 1 Cor. 1. 1: Σωσθένης ὁ ἀδελφός; Acts 9. 30: ἐπιγνόντες δὲ οἱ ἀδελφοὶ κατήγαγον αὐτὸν εἰς Καισαρίαν. The transition is easily seen — (1) member of the same family; (2) member of the same community (national); (3) member of the same community (spiritual).

ἀντίληψις—

I. In Class. Lit.—(1) receiving in exchange; (2) hold, support; (3) claim; (4) objection; (5) apprehension or perception.

II. In LXX., used to translate five Hebrew words meaning respectively—(a) arm, strength, aid; (b) shield; (c) defence, fortress; (d) strength, refuge; (e) help, aid. It is plain that the idea common to these words is "aid." All the passages occur in the Book of Psalms.

III. In N.T., 1 Cor. 12. 28: ἀντιλήψ(λημψ)εις, "helps." Mentioned among gifts bestowed on certain persons in the Christian Church, and classed with χαρίσματα ἰαμάτων, κυβερνήσεις κ.τ.λ. In Patristic Greek it is = help. Cf. Acts 20. 35: δεῖ ἀντιλαμβάνεσθαι τῶν ἀσθενούντων in a charge to the πρεσβύτεροι of Ephesus. The verb has an approach to this sense in several places in Thucyd., e.g. ii. 61. 3: τοῦ κοινοῦ τῆς σωτηρίας ἀντιλαμβάνεσθαι.

INFLUENCE OF SEPTUAGINT ON N.T. TERMS

διάβολος—
I. In Class. Lit.—(1) slanderous, Comic poets, Andoc. etc.; (2) slanderer, Pind., Xen., Arist.
II. In LXX. eighteen times out of twenty it translates שָׂטָן, "adversary," which, in these places, denotes "the adversary" κατ' ἐξοχήν, viz. Satan. Sixteen of these places are in Job and Zechariah.
III. In N.T. about thirty-five times in the above sense = the devil. Used also in the ordinary sense, 2 Tim. 3. 3: ἄστοργοι, ἄσπονδοι, διάβολοι. In the former sense, διάβολος always has the article.

δόξα—
I. In Class. Lit.—(1) expectation; (2) sentiment; (3) "opinion"; (4) estimation, good opinion; (5) credit.
II. In LXX. δόξα almost invariably translates one of three Hebrew words, but in different proportions. One of these, כָּבוֹד = honour, glory, splendour, it translates more than one hundred and fifty times. It is used next often to translate תִּפְאֶרֶת = glory, splendour, which it does about twenty times. Lastly, it is used nine times as = הוֹד, which denotes "majesty." By far its most common use is to translate the first word noted when used of God, and so = the glory with which God appears, an outward manifestation.
III. In N.T. fully one hundred and fifty times. Very frequently applied to God in the sense of "praise" and "honour." But a special sense, quite unheard of in Greek literature, is that which has arisen under the influence of the LXX., and which appears in places like Acts 22. 11: τῆς δόξης τοῦ φωτός; 2 Cor. 3. 7: διὰ τὴν δόξαν τοῦ προσώπου; 1 Cor. 15. 41: δόξα ἡλίου, σελήνης; Apoc. 21. 23: ἡ γὰρ δόξα τοῦ θεοῦ ἐφώτισεν κ.τ.λ. From this come further senses of "magnificence," "majesty," "exaltation"; the word, in short, assuming different shades of meaning according to the subjects to which it is applied.

ἔθνος—

I. In Class. Lit.—(1) band of men; (2) nation; (3) special caste, tribe.

II. In LXX. in an overwhelming number of cases to translate Heb. גּוֹי, which, in the first instance, is = a people (in general), but which in the *plural* is specially used of the *other* nations besides Israel, with an additional notion of their being outcasts and ignorant of the true religion. This always in LXX. = τὰ ἔθνη; Ps. 58. 9: ἐξουδενώσεις πάντα τὰ ἔθνη; Zech. 1. 15: ὀργὴν μεγάλην ὀργίζομαι ἐπὶ τὰ ἔθνη. Constantly used as opposed to λαός, which denotes Israel itself.

III. Accordingly, by a natural transition, in N.T., in such places as Luke 2. 32: φῶς εἰς ἀποκάλυψιν ἐθνῶν καὶ δόξαν λαοῦ σου Ἰσραήλ. So = pagans, Rom. 3. 29: ἢ Ἰουδαίων ὁ θεὸς μόνον; οὐχὶ καὶ ἐθνῶν; yet apparently always with a softened tone. So that it occurs = Gentile Christians, Rom. 15. 27: εἰ γὰρ τοῖς πνευματικοῖς αὐτῶν ἐκοινώνησαν τὰ ἔθνη, ὀφείλουσιν καὶ ἐν τοῖς σαρκικοῖς λειτουργῆσαι αὐτοῖς. By Aristides (160 A.D.), τὰ ἔθνη are opposed to the Greeks.

εἰρήνη—

I. In Class. Lit. usu. = "peace," as opp. to "war." But modifications of this, as Plat. *Sympos.* 189 B: ἐάν τι γελοῖον εἴπῃς ἐξόν σοι ἐν εἰρήνῃ λέγειν, just as would naturally come about in language.

II. In LXX. it translates more than one hundred and fifty times Heb. שָׁלוֹם, which has for its root-idea, physical soundness of body, health, and so reaches its metaphorical and ruling sense of security and tranquillity of state, prosperity of mind and body, welfare. From this comes to it in a secondary way the meaning of "peace" as opp. to "war," because in times of peace things are secure and tranquil. It translates six times Heb. בֶּטַח = security, as springing from confidence in some person or circumstance.

III. In N.T. the Class. meaning is often found. But other senses predominate. (a) Concord in private life, e.g. Luke 12. 51: δοκεῖτε ὅτι εἰρήνην παρεγενόμην δοῦναι . . .; οὐχὶ λέγω ὑμῖν ἀλλ' ἢ διαμερισμόν, etc. etc. (b) Usage based on LXX. = happiness or prosperity. About thirty times in phrase εἰρήνη ὑμῖν. (Perhaps this has a tinge of additional signification in the apostolic writings.) Acts 16. 36: πορεύεσθε ἐν εἰρήνῃ; Matt. 10. 13: ἡ εἰρήνη ὑμῶν πρὸς ὑμᾶς ἐπιστραφήτω, i.e. "your wish of prosperity." (c) Special Christian sense, which is an extension of (b) = rest of soul in God through Christ. John 16. 33: ταῦτα λελάληκα ὑμῖν ἵνα ἐν ἐμοὶ εἰρήνην ἔχητε. So appar. in places like Phil. 4. 7: ἡ εἰρήνη τοῦ θεοῦ; Acts 10. 36: εὐαγγελίζεσθαι εἰρήνην διὰ Ἰησοῦ. Prob. this sense also in the salutations at the beginning and end of the Epistles. In late Byzantine Greek it came to be a technical term in phrases like δοῦναι τὴν εἰρήνην = to say εἰρήνη πᾶσιν.

ἐκκλησία—

I. In Class. Lit. = the legislative assembly.

II. In LXX. used almost invariably to translate Heb. קָהָל, which denotes specially "the congregation of the Israelites assembled." Josh. 8. 35: ὃ οὐκ ἀνέγνω εἰς τὰ ὦτα πάσης τῆς ἐκκλησίας; 2 Chron. 29. 31: καὶ ἀνήνεγκεν ἡ ἐκκλησία θυσίας.

III. In N.T. the usage of the LXX. determines the sense of the word, which is = the public gathering of Christians viewed externally as met for a common purpose, or organised with a common aim, or, viewed from an inward standpoint as a spiritual corporation. Rom. 16. 5: τὴν κατ' οἶκον αὐτῶν ἐκκλησίαν; Acts 5. 11: καὶ ἐγένετο φόβος μέγας ἐφ' ὅλην τὴν ἐκκλησίαν; Gal. 1. 13: ἐδίωκον τὴν ἐκκλησίαν τοῦ θεοῦ.

Used in writers like Polybius of any public meeting, e.g. Polyb. 23. 10. 10: ὁ Κ. ἠξίου τοὺς πολλοὺς αὐτῷ συναγαγεῖν εἰς ἐκκλησίαν.

κακία—

I. In Class. Lit.—(1) badness, as opp. to ἀρετή; (2) cowardice; (3) vice, occas. = dishonour.

II. In LXX. κακία, in an overwhelming majority of instances translates Heb. רָעָה, which means (a) moral evil; (b) external evil, evil circumstances. In at least half of these cases it is used in sense (b) = "trouble," "misfortune."

III. In N.T., along with the ordinary senses, there is a use based on the LXX. in Matt. 6. 34: ἀρκετὸν τῇ ἡμέρᾳ ἡ κακία αὐτῆς. This sense, however, may have been common in spoken Greek. Cf. Dionys. Hal. Antiq. *Rom.* vi. 370: πᾶσαν κακίαν καὶ διαφορὰν καὶ ἀνατροπὴν πόλεως. Chrysos. vii. 279 C uses it = ταλαιπωρία.

κληρονόμος—

I. In Class. Lit. = heir, inheritor.

II. In LXX. it translates Heb. יָרַשׁ, which means (1) possessor, Judg. 18. 7: κληρονόμος ἐκπιέζων θησαυροῦ; Jer. 8. 10: δώσω καὶ τοὺς ἀγροὺς αὐτῶν τοῖς κληρονόμοις. (2) Heir, 2 Sam. 14. 7: καὶ ἐξαροῦμεν καί γε τὸν κληρονόμον ὑμῶν, etc.

III. In N.T.—(a) often in ord. sense of "heir"; (b) spiritual sense, of those who have a right to spiritual privileges through being sons of God, Rom. 8. 17: εἰ δὲ τέκνα, καὶ κληρονόμοι· κληρονόμοι μὲν θεοῦ κ.τ.λ. (c) As in (1) under the LXX., without the idea of inheritance = possessor, Heb. 6. 17: βουλόμενος ὁ θεὸς ἐπιδεῖξαι τοῖς κληρονόμοις τῆς ἐπαγγελίας; Heb. 11. 7: τῆς κατὰ πίστιν δικαιοσύνης ἐγένετο κληρόνομος.

κρίσις—

I. In Class. Lit. = (1) judgment, in various senses; (2) trial; (3) condemnation; (4) quarrel; (5) event or issue.

II. In LXX. κρίσις is used in the vast majority of cases to translate Heb. מִשְׁפָּט, meaning (1) judgment, sentence; (2) that which is according to law, right. And so we often find it joined with δικαιοσύνη (often), ἔλεος (Ps. 100. 1), ἀλήθεια (Ps. 110. 6), ἐλεημοσύνη. God is said· ἀγαπᾶν κρίσιν. In one place it translates the Heb. word for "righteousness."

III. In the N.T. there is a class of passages where this sense must be adopted. These are in Matt. and Luke; e.g. Luke 11. 42: καὶ παρέρχεσθε τὴν κρίσιν καὶ τὴν ἀγάπην τοῦ θεοῦ; Matt. 23. 23: τὰ βαρύτερα τοῦ νόμου τὴν κρίσιν καὶ τὸ ἔλεος καὶ τὴν πίστιν. Here evidently the word denotes a moral quality of God, namely, "justice."

παιδεία—

I. In Class. Lit.—(1) education; (2) its result = mental culture. Several minor meanings.

II. Out of forty-seven occurrences in the LXX., thirty-six are a translation of Heb. מוּסָר, which usually means "correction," sometimes "admonition" or "discipline." The Heb. verb from which the noun is derived means, as a rule, "chastise," though sometimes "admonish." The word is specially used in the O.T. of chastisement on God's side by sorrow and evil, often also of a father's chastening of his son.

παιδεία translates no other word more than once or twice. We find it in the LXX. parallel with ἔλεγχος, θλῖψις, μάστιγες.

III. In the N.T. it occurs in four places in Hebrews. One of these is a quotation from the LXX., Prov. 3. 11: μὴ ὀλιγώρει παιδείας κυρίου. In all of these it means "chastisement." It is found also in two other passages, Eph. 6. 4: ἐκτρέφετε [τὰ τέκνα] ἐν παιδείᾳ καὶ νουθεσίᾳ κυρίου; 2 Tim. 3. 16: πᾶσα γραφὴ ... ὠφέλιμος πρὸς διδασκαλίαν, πρὸς ἐλεγμόν, πρὸς ἐπανόρθωσιν, πρὸς παιδείαν κ.τ.λ. In this last place it seems as if παιδεία might be taken in the sense already quoted, seeing it is joined with words so strong as ἐπανόρθωσις and ἐλεγμός. So very probably in Ephesians also, where it is joined with νουθεσία, a word which has often a more or less drastic sense. Ellicott quotes Grotius *ad loc.*: "παιδεία hic significare videtur institutionem per pœnas; νουθεσία autem est ea institutio quæ fit verbis." A hint of this sense in Polyb. 2. 9. 6, when he speaks of people as παιδεύεσθαι πρὸς τὸ μέλλον, which Schweighäuser translates: "recevoir une bonne leçon pour l'avenir."

In Philo still = education. In late Byzantine, such as Theophanes Continuatus = chastisement.

πάροικος—

I. In Class. Lit. = neighbouring, dwelling near.

II. In LXX. used twenty-four times. Eleven times of these it translates Heb. גר, meaning "sojourner," "person living out of his own country." Ten times it translates Heb. תּוֹשָׁב, denoting an "emigrant sojourning in a strange country, where he is not naturalised." It is joined in Gen. 23. 4 with παρεπίδημος. It occurs several times in combination with ἐν γῇ ἀλλοτρίᾳ.

III. In N.T. four times.—(1) Acts 7. 6, quotation from the LXX.: πάροικον ἐν γῇ ἀλλοτρίᾳ, where = sojourner; (2) Acts 7. 29: πάροικος ἐν γῇ Μαδιάμ; (3) Eph. 2. 19, joined with ξένοι; (4) 1 Pet. 2. 11, joined with παρεπίδημος.

This shows that the use is based on that of the LXX. (3) and (4) are a Christian extension of the meaning as found in the LXX. They are both metaphorical uses of the word.

The word [1] denoted, in several eastward regions, e.g. Carpathos, Ilium Novum, etc. (*C.I.G.* 3595, etc.), the same thing as the Attic μέτοικος.

The Christian sense is clearly seen in *Epist. ad Diognet.* v. 5: πατρίδας οἰκοῦσιν (*sc.* οἱ Χριστιανοί) ἰδίας ἀλλ' ὡς πάροικοι; Polycarp, *Ep. ad Philipp. Inscript.*: Πολύκαρπος . . . τῇ ἐκκλησίᾳ τοῦ θεοῦ τῇ παροικούσῃ Φιλίπποις.

σάρξ—

I. In Class. Lit. = "flesh" in the various ordinary senses of the word.

II. In the LXX. σάρξ, practically without exception, trans-

[1] So Thayer in Grimm.

lates Heb. בָּשָׂר = "flesh." But besides the ordinary sense, this word has several special meanings. (1) = living creature (usu. man). So σάρξ occurs in this sense, e.g. Gen. 7. 21: ἀπέθανε πᾶσα σὰρξ κινουμένη ἐπὶ τῆς γῆς; Deut. 5. 26: τίς γὰρ σὰρξ ἥτις ἤκουσε φωνὴν θεοῦ ζῶντος; Ps. 55. 4: οὐ φοβηθήσομαι τί ποιήσει μοι σάρξ. (2) = physical nature or relationship. A curious mixed signification, e.g. Gen. 37. 26: ὅτι ἀδελφὸς ἡμῶν καὶ σὰρξ ἡμῶν ἐστίν; Judg. 9. 2: σὰρξ ὑμῶν εἰμὶ ἐγώ.

III. In N.T. an enormous widening and deepening of meaning, so that it has both the ordinary senses, a variety of special theological meanings, and also one or two which come through the LXX. Its special theological meanings start from the notion of σάρξ as opposed to πνεῦμα, man's earthly nature apart from divine influence. Two senses are immediately connected with the influence of the LXX. (1) About eleven instances of σάρξ in the sense of "living being." Very generally in the combination πᾶσα σάρξ, e.g. Matt. 24. 22: οὐκ ἂν ἐσώθη πᾶσα σάρξ. Perhaps in the phrase, John 1. 14: ὁ λόγος σὰρξ ἐγένετο. So often (2) of physical nature and relationship, e.g. Rom. 1. 3: γενόμενος ἐκ σπέρματος Δαυεὶδ κατὰ σάρκα; Heb. 12. 9: οἱ τῆς σαρκὸς ἡμῶν πατέρες.

So Clem. Rom. 1. 32. 2: ἐξ αὐτοῦ . . . Ἰησοῦς τὸ κατὰ σάρκα. Even Plut. ii. 159 B uses σάρξ as = body, showing the tendency in the word.

σωτήρ—

I. In Class. Lit. = saviour, deliverer, guardian.
II. In LXX. used twenty times. In eighteen of these it is employed of God.
III. In N.T. constantly, and always either of God or Christ, especially in the sense of saving from sin.

Verbs

ἀναφέρω—

I. In Class. Lit. = (1) bring or carry up; (2) sustain; (3)

bring back; (4) refer; and various other subordinate senses.

II. In LXX.—(1) ordinary senses, a very few times; (2) about ninety times in ritual sense = offer. Especially in the phrase: ἀναφέρειν ὁλοκαυτώματα, ὁλοκαυτώσεις.

III. In N.T.—(1) bring up, three places; (2) sustain, once, Heb. 9. 28; (3) = (2) of LXX., *e.g.* Heb. 7. 27: πρότερον ὑπὲρ τῶν ἰδίων ἁμαρτιῶν θυσίας ἀναφέρειν; 1 Pet. 2. 5: ἀνενέγκαι πνευματικὰς θυσίας εὐπροσδέκτους; and other three places.

In Demos. 1030. 13 it is used = contribute: ἀναφέρειν εἰς τὸ κοινόν. This seems to prepare the way for the prevailing sense in the LXX.

ἀποκαλύπτω—

I. In Class. Lit. = disclose, reveal.

II. In LXX.—(1) ordinary senses; (2) special sense of God revealing hidden things to men, Dan. 2. 28: ἀλλ' ἔστι θεὸς ἐν οὐρανῷ ὁ ἀποκαλύπτων μυστήρια; 1 Sam. 3. 21: ἀπεκαλύφθη κύριος πρὸς Σαμουήλ; Isa. 56. 1: τὸ ἔλεός μου ἀποκαλυφθῆναι.

III. In N.T.—(1) ordinary senses; (2) = (2) of LXX., Matt. 11. 25: ἀπεκάλυψας αὐτὰ νηπίοις; Rom. 1. 18: ἀποκαλύπτεται γὰρ ὀργὴ θεοῦ; Eph. 3. 5: νῦν ἀπεκαλύφθη τοῖς ἁγίοις ἀποστόλοις, etc.

δικαιόω—

I. In Class. Lit.—(1) make or deem right; (2) do a man right or justice. So Hdt., Thuycd., Soph.

II. In LXX. it translates Heb. צדק in the Hiph'il mood. This verb has two main senses—(1) Exhibit one to be righteous, *e.g.* Ezek. 16. 51: ἐδικαίωσας τὰς ἀδελφάς σου ἐν πάσαις ταῖς ἀνομίαις σου; Jer. 3. 11: ἐδικαίωσε τὴν ψυχὴν αὐτοῦ Ἰσραὴλ ἀπὸ τῆς ἀσυνθέτου Ἰούδα. (2) Pronounce righteous, *e.g.* Deut. 25. 1: καὶ δικαιώσουσι τὸν δίκαιον; Ex. 23. 7: καὶ οὐ δικαιώσεις τὸν ἀσεβῆ ἕνεκεν δώρων; Isa. 50. 8: ἐγγίζει ὁ δικαιώσας με.

III. In N.T. the chief meanings are—(1) = (1) under LXX.,

INFLUENCE OF SEPTUAGINT ON N.T. TERMS 105

e.g. Luke 7. 35 : ἡ σοφία ἐδικαιώθη ἀπὸ τῶν τέκνων αὐτῆς. (2)=(2) under LXX., *e.g.* Luke 10. 29 : ὁ δὲ θέλων δικαιῶσαι ἑαυτόν ; Rom. 2. 13 : οἱ ποιηταὶ τοῦ νόμου δικαιωθήσονται. (3) A special sense in the technical phraseology of St. Paul, in which it = God's declaring those persons righteous in His eyes who put faith in Christ. This is simply a Christian expansion of (2), *e.g.* Rom. 3. 30 : ὃς δικαιώσει περιτομὴν ἐκ πίστεως, *et passim*. So in Justin M. *Fragg.* p. 566 (Otto's edition): δεύτερον ἀγαθὸν τὸ δικαιωθῆναι.

In Church-Greek δικαιόω came to be a technical term, used of the decrees of Councils, *e.g.* Concil. Nicæn. Can. 17 : ἐδικαίωσεν ἡ ἁγία καὶ μεγάλη σύνοδος.

ἐπισκέπτομαι (ἐπισκοπέω)—

I. In Class. Lit.—(1) inspect ; (2) visit ; (3) consider.

II. In LXX.—(1) Visit, *e.g.* Jud. 15. 1 : καὶ ἐπεσκέψατο Σαμψὼν τὴν γυναῖκα. (2) Far more freq. = care for, visit, in the sense of provide for, *e.g.* Ex. 4. 31 : ἐχάρη ὅτι ἐπεσκέψατο ὁ θεὸς τοὺς υἱούς ; Ps. 8. 5 : τί ἐστιν ἄνθρωπος ὅτι ἐπισκέπτῃ αὐτόν. (3) Visit with punishment, *e.g.* Jer. 9. 25 : καὶ ἐπισκέψομαι ἐπὶ πάντας περιτετμημένους ἀκροβυστίας αὐτῶν ; Ps. 88. 32 : ἐπισκέψομαι ἐν ῥάβδῳ τὰς ἀνομίας αὐτῶν. (4) Often = number the people.

III. In N.T.—(1) = (1) under LXX., yet with a shade of (2) implied, *e.g.* Jas. 1. 27 : ἐπισκέπτεσθαι ὀρφανούς ; Matt. 25. 36 : ἠσθένησα καὶ ἐπεσκέψασθέ με. (2) = (2) of LXX., *e.g.* Luke 7. 16 : ἐπεσκέψατο ὁ θεὸς τὸν λαόν ; Luke 1. 78 : διὰ σπλάγχνα ἐλέους θεοῦ ἡμῶν ἐν οἷς ἐπεσκέψατο ἡμᾶς ἀνατολὴ ἐξ ὕψους.

Often in Plutarch of "visiting" the sick.

εὐλογέω—

I. In Class. Lit. = praise, speak well of, Tragg., Aristoph.

II. In LXX.—(1) Ordinary sense = praise, *e.g.* Deut. 8. 10 : καὶ εὐλογήσεις κύριον τὸν θεόν σου ; 2 Chron. 30. 27 : ἀνέστησαν δὲ ἱερεῖς καὶ εὐλόγησαν τὸν θεόν. (2) Invoke blessings on, e.g. Gen. 24. 60: εὐλόγησαν Ῥεβέκκαν καὶ εἶπαν αὐτῇ; Num. 23. 20: ἰδοὺ εὐλογεῖν παρείλημμαι, εὐλογήσω. (3) Bestow blessings on (used of God), e.g. Josh. 17. 4: λαὸς πολύς εἰμι καὶ ὁ θεός με εὐλόγησε; Ps. 44. 3: διὰ τοῦτο εὐλόγησέ σε ὁ θεὸς εἰς τὸν αἰῶνα; and so often.

III. In N.T.—(1) Ordinary sense, e.g. Jas. 3. 9: ἐν αὐτῇ εὐλογοῦμεν τὸν κύριον. (2) = (2) of LXX., e.g. Luke 6. 28: εὐλογεῖτε τοὺς καταρωμένους ὑμᾶς; Heb. 7. 9: ὁ συναντήσας Ἀβραάμ . . . καὶ εὐλογήσας αὐτόν. (3) = (3) of LXX., e.g. Acts 3. 26: εὐλογοῦντα ὑμᾶς κ.τ.λ.; Eph. 1. 3: ὁ εὐλογήσας ἡμᾶς ἐν πάσῃ εὐλογίᾳ πνευματικῇ. Strange use in Church-Greek = marry. Gregent. 585 A, εὐλογεῖσθαι = be married. Philo knows the word, but prefers to use ἐπαινεῖν, and the like.

πειράζω—

I. In Class. Lit. Not often in good authors, who prefer πειράω. (1) Make proof of, Hom.; (2) attempt, try, later writers; (3) tempt, Apoll. Rhod. 3. 10.

II. In LXX. It translates Heb. נִסָּה, which is = put to the test, in a good sense or a bad. (1) Said of God as bringing calamity on men to test the trustworthiness of their faith, e.g. Gen. 22. 1: ὁ θεὸς ἐπείραζε τὸν Ἀβραάμ; Deut. 13. 3: πειράζει κύριος ὁ θεὸς ὑμῶν ὑμᾶς. (2) Used of men in relation to God as testing God's character, but in the bad sense, from the point of view of distrust, and so causing Him to prove Himself either by showing kindness or punishment, e.g. Ex. 17. 2: τί λοιδορεῖσθέ μοι καὶ τί πειράζετε κύριον; Ps. 105. 15: ἐπείρασαν τὸν θεὸν ἐν ἀνύδρῳ; Isa. 7. 12: οὐ μὴ αἰτήσω οὐδὲ μὴ πειράσω κύριον.

III. In N.T. the Class. meanings occur several times. But usu. those derived through the LXX. (1) = (1) of the LXX., e.g. 1 Cor. 10. 13: πιστὸς δὲ ὁ θεὸς ὃς οὐκ ἐάσει ὑμᾶς πειρασθῆναι ὑπὲρ ὃ δύνασθε; Heb. 11. 17: πίστει προσενήνοχεν Ἀβραὰμ τὸν Ἰσαὰκ πειραζόμενος. (2) = (2) under LXX., e.g. Acts 15. 10: τί πειράζετε τὸν

θεόν; 1 Cor. 10. 9: μηδὲ πειράζωμεν τὸν κύριον καθώς
τινες αὐτῶν ἐπείρασαν (v.l. ἐξεπείρασαν).
In this second sense, cf. Hdt. vi. 86. 3: ἡ δὲ Πυθίη ἔφη τὸ
πειρηθῆναι τοῦ θεοῦ καὶ τὸ ποιῆσαι ἴσον δύνασθαι, where
πειράομαι appears to be used in a very analogous sense.
Cf. Protevangel. Jacobi, 20: οὐαὶ τῇ ἀπιστίᾳ μου ὅτι
ἐξεπείρασα θεὸν ζῶντα; Strabo, 16. 4. 24, uses πειράζεσθαι
in the sense of being afflicted.
Plut. ii. 230 A = *examinari* (Wyttenb.).

πορεύομαι—

I. In Class. Lit. = "go," and many subordinate senses.
II. In LXX.—(1) Ord. sense in a great many places. (2)
Vanish, *e.g.* Ps. 78. 39: ἐμνήσθη ὅτι σάρξ εἰσι, πνεῦμα
πορευόμενον καὶ οὐκ ἐπιστρέφον. From this comes
further the sense of "die," as Gen. 15. 2, where the
common Heb. verb for "go" is used. (3) Live, follow
a manner of life. Very common. Deut. 19. 9:
πορεύεσθε ἐν πάσαις ταῖς ὁδοῖς αὐτοῦ; Ps. 14. 2:
πορευόμενος ἄμωμος.
III. In N.T.—(1) Usual sense often. (2) = (2) of the LXX.,
e.g. Luke 22. 22: ὁ υἱὸς μὲν τοῦ ἀνθρώπου κατὰ τὸ
ὡρισμένον πορεύεται. This, modelled on Heb. use of the
verb הָלַךְ = Greek οἴχεσθαι. (3) = (3) of LXX., *e.g.*
Acts 9. 31: πορευόμεναι τῷ φόβῳ τοῦ κυρίου; 1 Pet.
4. 3: πεπορευμένους ἐν ἀσελγείαις.

A shade of similar meaning in Soph. *O. T.* 883: εἰ δέ τις
ὑπέροπτα χερσὶν ἢ λόγῳ πορεύεται.

φωτίζω—

I. In Class. Lit. Only in late writers, Theophr., Aristot.,
Diodor., Plut., Polyb. (1) Give or transmit light; (2)
light up (of the sun); (3) metaph. = make known,
bring to light.
II. In LXX. It usually translates Heb. הֵאִיר (Hiph'il of
אוֹר), meaning "enlighten" "illuminate"; or הוֹרָה (Hiph.
of יָרָה) = teach. Not found in its literal sense. Always
= enlighten mentally (= educate, teach) or spiritually,

e.g. Ps. 12. 4: φώτισον τοὺς ὀφθαλμούς μου; Ps. 118. 129: ἡ δήλωσις τῶν λόγων σου φωτιεῖ (this example shows the process in the word); Judg. 13. 8: φωτισάτω ἡμᾶς, τί ποιήσομεν τῷ παιδαρίῳ; 2 Kings 12. 2: πάσας τὰς ἡμέρας ἃς ἐφώτισεν αὐτόν.

III. In N.T. It has senses (2) and (3) under I. Also the additional peculiar signification found in the LXX. (1) = (2) under I., e.g. Luke 11. 36: ὅταν ὁ λύχνος τῇ ἀστραπῇ φωτίζῃ σε; Apoc. 18. 1, etc. (2) = (3) under I., e.g. 1 Cor. 4. 5: ὁ κύριος ὃς καὶ φωτίσει τὰ κρυπτὰ τοῦ σκότους; 2 Tim. 1. 10: φωτίσαντος δὲ ζωὴν καὶ ἀφθαρσίαν διὰ τοῦ εὐαγγελίου. (3) = usage of LXX. pecul. to Bibl. Greek, Heb. 6. 4: τοὺς ἅπαξ φωτισθέντας; Eph. 3. 9: φωτίσαι τίς ἡ οἰκονομία τοῦ μυστηρίου; Eph. 1. 18: πεφωτισμένους τοὺς ὀφθαλμοὺς τῆς καρδίας ὑμῶν.

The second use quoted under the N.T. is found in Polyb. 30. 8. 1: γράμματα ἑαλωκότα καὶ πεφωτισμένα; Lucian. *Cal. non tem.* 32: πεφωτισμένων τῶν πραγμάτων ὑπὸ τῆς ἀληθείας. So Plut. ii. 902 B: φωτίζουσα τὰ νοούμενα. Diog. Laert. 1. 57 uses the verb of bringing an unknown writer before the public. Justin M. has the special N.T. use, *Tryph.* 122: τῷ ὄντι δὲ εἰς ἡμᾶς εἴρηται τοὺς διὰ Ἰησοῦ πεφωτισμένους. An interesting derivative from this sense is its technical meaning in Church-Greek = baptize, e.g. Justin M. *Apol.* 61 E: ὁ φωτιζόμενος λούεται; 65 C: εὐχὰς ποιησάμενοι ὑπὲρ τοῦ φωτισθέντος.

With the exception of words formed in direct imitation of Hebrew expressions by the writers of the LXX., and found also in the New Testament, which will be considered immediately, that class of terms which has just been illustrated is the clearest instance of a direct influence of the LXX. on the vocabulary of the New Testament.

This at once points out close-drawn limits. For even

among the words annotated, there are at least some whose presence in the New Testament may *not* be due to the usage of the LXX. at all. Several of the "Biblical" meanings, though apparently moulded by the Greek of the Old Testament, may have been common enough in the spoken language as found in Egypt, Asia Minor, and Syria. When it is borne in mind that there are literally almost no remains of the later spoken language except the LXX. and the New Testament, in addition to the Comic writers, and when, as has been indicated under the words themselves, distinct traces of cognate senses occur in stray writers of the κοινή, the supposition gains colour. At any rate, it shows us that we are not at liberty to make dogmatic assertions even in that sphere of the New Testament vocabulary where the influence of the LXX. appears most powerful, the sphere of religious and theological terms. Besides, the writers of the New Testament were themselves "Hebrews of the Hebrews," and so their language must always have a Jewish tinge, whether this is due to a stereotyped Judæo-Greek formed by the LXX., or whether it is, as seems to be the case, the natural colour given to the spoken Greek of the day by its passage through the Semitic mind.

One other fact must be noted. The special theological terms of the New Testament are at most *connected* with, not derived from, the usage of the LXX. The latter, as a rule, simply affords a starting-point for the creation of the language of Christian theology.

CHAPTER IX

Discussion of various Classes of Words in the New Testament, which either in themselves or by their particular Uses suggest a Connection with the Septuagint

It has been thought advisable to place the more strictly religious and theological terms which have reached their technical sense through the influence of the LXX., and then of the New Testament, in a class by themselves. In this section we must examine several other groups of words occurring in the New Testament, which either in themselves or by their particular uses there suggest, with more or less probability, a definite connection with the LXX.

We begin with those whose derivation from that source is most probable.

1. Actual Hebrew words occurring in the New Testament.

These are of various forms, some being mere transliterations, as $\sigma\alpha\beta\alpha\omega\theta$; others undergoing distinct changes, either in the body of the word, as $\sigma\iota\kappa\lambda o\varsigma$, or merely in regard to endings, as $\kappa\acute{o}\rho o\varsigma$. There are about thirteen Hebraic words common to the LXX. and New Testament, six of which occur also in Philo. Examples of them have been given on p. 44. And certainly one is inclined, at first sight, to say that these *must* have come through the LXX., especially as the majority of them are real Biblical words connected with the written history of the Israelites, *e.g.* μάννα, πάσχα, χερουβείν. But it is by no means unlikely that, from the first days of Jewish settlements in Greek-speaking countries, these words of ritual and worship were in common circulation. At least, the tendency shown by such formations is common, for in the New Testament we find twenty Hebrew and Aramaic words which do *not* occur in the LXX., *e.g.* ζιζάνιον, μαμωνᾶς, ῥακά, ὡσαννά.

2. A class far more interesting and of far greater importance, for the vocabulary of the New Testament is that consisting of words expressing ideas and customs specially Jewish, which were employed by the writers of the LXX. as literal translations of the Hebrew terms, or were formed by them on the analogy of these terms. They occur, in considerable numbers, in the New Testament. Here, again, it appears certainly probable that these words gained currency through the influence of the LXX., and so passed into the vocabulary of the New Testament. Most of them are not found elsewhere in literature. We shall illustrate this class fully, as it is of the first importance in connection with our special subject. Typical instances will be given.

Nouns

ἀκροβυστία—
  A word unknown to the Greeks = ἀκροποσθία. Some scholars favour the hypothesis that πόσθη was pronounced βύστη by Alexandrians. But Cremer seems

nearer the mark in holding that the word was certainly formed by the Jews, probably with the Heb. = בֹּשֶׁת (= "shame") in view.

I. In the LXX. always in the phys. sense = *præputium*. When the Hebrew word which it translates is figurative, as often in O.T., the LXX. has σκληροκαρδία.

II. In N.T.—(1) Phys. sense constantly, e.g. Acts 11. 3: ἄνδρας ἀκροβυστίαν ἔχοντας. (2) In the abstract = Gentiles, Eph. 2. 11, etc. (3) Metaphor. sense, e.g. Col. 2. 13: τῇ ἀκροβυστίᾳ τῆς σαρκὸς ὑμῶν.

ἐπισκοπή—

I. In LXX. almost invariably translates derivatives of Heb. verb פָּקַד = (1) visit, investigate; (2) oversee.

(1) *E.g.* Jer. 8. 12: ἐν καιρῷ ἐπισκοπῆς αὐτῶν πεσοῦνται.

(2) *E.g.* Num. 4. 16: ἡ ἐπισκοπὴ ὅλης τῆς σκηνῆς.

Also used (3) of the numbering of Israel. *E.g.* Ex. 30. 12: λάβῃς τὸν συλλογισμὸν ἐν τῇ ἐπισκοπῇ αὐτῶν.

II. In N.T.—(1) Visitation, e.g. 1 Pet. 2. 12: ἐν ἡμέρᾳ ἐπισκοπῆς. (2) Overseership, 1 Tim. 3. 1: εἴ τις ἐπισκοπῆς ὀρέγεται κ.τ.λ.

Cf. Luc. *Dial. Deor.* 20. 6: εἰς ἐπισκοπὴν τοῦ παιδός, in a colloquial sense.

More common in the LXX. is ἐπίσκεψις, in senses (1) and (3).

ἐφημερία—

I. In LXX. = (1) The daily service of the priests in the temple, e.g. Neh. 13. 30: καὶ ἔστησεν ἐφημερίας τοῖς ἱερεῦσιν. (2) The separate groups of priests who performed this service, e.g. 2 Chron. 5. 10: οὐκ ἦσαν διατεταγμένοι εἰς ἐφημερίας.

II. In N.T. = (2) Luke 1. 5: Ζαχαρίας ἐξ ἐφημερίας Ἀβιά. Joseph. *De Vita sua* 1, uses ἐφημερίς as = (2)

> Suidas: ἐφημερία· ἡ πατριά. λέγεται δὲ καὶ ἡ τῆς ἡμέρας λειτουργία.

Cf mod. Greek, ἐφημέριος = priest.

ἱλαστήριον—
I. In LXX. practically always = Heb. כַּפֹּרֶת, denoting the lid or covering of the ark. A great number of instances in Exodus and Leviticus.
II. In N.T. used in Heb. 9. 5 in the above sense. In Rom. 3. 25 it may be either (1) as above, (2) expiatory sacrifice, or (3) offering, as afterwards in Dion Chrysost. and the Byzantine writers.
Also in Philo, ii. 150. 2. Used as an adj. in Joseph. *Antiq.* 16. 7. 1: μνῆμα ἱλαστήριον.

καταπέτασμα—
= Ord. Gk. παραπέτασμα.
I. In LXX. used often of the two veils or curtains in the temple at Jerusalem.
II. In N.T. always of the innermost of the two curtains, Matt. 27. 51; Luke 23. 45; Heb. 9. 3. Also figuratively of the body of Christ, Heb. 10. 20.
Found also in Joseph., Philo, Apocr., and Aristeas. Apparently entirely confined to Jewish usage.

ματαιότης—
I. In LXX. almost always = what is evanescent, vain, empty; so = falsehood, emptiness, vanity. Especially following the meaning of the Heb. שָׁוְא, which it translates = emptiness, in the sense of wickedness or impiety. Numerous instances of this.
II. In N.T. 2 Pet. 2. 18, appar. = worthlessness. This sense prob. suits Eph. 14. 17: ἐν ματαιότητι τοῦ νοὸς αὐτῶν. The other passage, Rom. 8. 20, seems to require some such meaning as "fruitlessness," which is, of course, closely connected with those above.
Occurs in no secular author except Pollux, 6. 134.

ὁλοκαύτωμα—
I. In LXX. translates usually Heb. עֹלָה, meaning "whole burnt-offering."
II. So also in N.T. Mark 12. 33; Heb. 10. 6.

Phrynichus mentions in his Appendix, p. 51, the forms μηροκαυτεῖν, ἱεροκαυτεῖν, ὁλοκαυτεῖν, which last is only written so in Xen. *Anab.* 7. 8. 4; Joseph. *Antiq.* 3. 9. 171. Sometimes ὁλοκαυτοῦν, Xen. *Cyr.* 8. 3. 24; Joseph. *Antiq.* 1. 13. 40. Doubtful verb-form in Plut. ii. 694 B. The noun occurs once in Philo. Joseph. twice uses ὁλοκαύτωσις. A form ὁλοκαυτίζω is also found.

παντοκράτωρ—

I. In LXX. a great many times. Always = Lord of Hosts.
II. In N.T., nine times in Apocalypse, once in 2 Cor. in sense of "Almighty." Exceedingly common in all the earliest Christian literature (cf. numerous examples in Harnack's notes on I. Clemens ad Corinthios).

In the Greek Anthology, iv. 151.

πατριάρχης—

A word presumably formed by the LXX. on the analogy of Heb. expressions with ראשׁ ("head") and שַׂר ("prince"), denoting leaders of tribes or families. About six times in the LXX. Directly transferred to the N.T., *e.g.* Acts 2. 29; Heb. 7. 4.

"Compounds in -αρχος usu. exchange this ending for -αρχης in the N.T. and late Greek. That -αρχης was the usual termination in the apostolic age seems a legitimate inference from the fact that the Romans, in translating these words into Latin, used this or a similar form, *e.g.* 'Alabarches,' Juv. i. 130; 'Tetrarches,' Hor. *Sat.* i. 3. 12" (Winer).

προσευχή—

I. In LXX. numerous instances in the sense of "prayer."
II. In N.T.—(1) prayer, many instances; (2) place of prayer, Acts 16. 16: πορευομένων ἡμῶν εἰς τὴν προσευχήν. This last use in Philo, ii. 523. 22, etc.; Juv. *Sat.* i. 3. 296, "proseucha"; Joseph. *Vita*, 54; several Inscr.; Cleomedes, 71. 16.

προσήλυτος—

I. In LXX. almost always translates Heb. גֵּר = foreigner, alien. So also in Philo.

II. In N.T. three or four times, and always in the technical sense of one who has left some Gentile religion for Judaism. Literally = Lat. "*advena*." Winer[1] says on the form: "The verbal προσήλυτος is immediately connected with such forms as ἔπηλυς, μέτηλυς, and is an extended formation, of which we find no examples in Greek authors."

ῥαντισμός—

I. In LXX. in four places, *e.g.* in phrase ὕδωρ ῥαντισμοῦ = water for sprinkling, so as to remove defilement. Always = sprinkling.

II. In N.T. same sense. Used always with αἷμα. A technical term of ritual in the LXX. Not found in any secular author. The nearest approach is ῥάντισις in Achmes, a late writer of the Christian era.

σκληροκαρδία—

I. In LXX. Deut. 10. 16: καὶ περιτεμεῖσθε τὴν σκληροκαρδίαν αὐτῶν; Jer. 4. 4 in the same connection.

II. In N.T. three times in the same sense.

The adj. σκληροκάρδιος occurs in several places in the LXX.

Adjectives

ἀνθρωπάρεσκος—

I. In LXX. Ps. 52. 6, where it has nothing to correspond to it in the Hebrew text.

II. In N.T. Eph. 6. 6: μὴ κατ' ὀφθαλμοδουλίαν ὡς ἀνθρωπάρεσκοι. So Col. 3. 22.

Lobeck compares αὐτάρεσκος, Apoll. *de Conjunct.* 504, and ὀχλοάρεσκος in Hesych.

The adj. occurs in Theophil. 3. 14.

The noun is found in Justin Martyr.

[1] P. 120.

λαξευτός. λᾶς + ξέω = hewn out of stone, of hewn stone.
I. In LXX. Deut. 4. 49: τὴν λαξευτήν. In apposition to a proper name.
II. In N.T., Luke 23. 53: μνῆμα λαξευτόν. Also in apocryphal Gospel of Nicodemus. Aquila has it several times in the Pentateuch.
The verb λαξεύω occurs twice in Exodus, and once in Isaiah and Deuteronomy.
λάξευσις, Schol. ad Theoc. 6. 18.
λαξευτής, Manetho, 1. 77.

μοιχαλίς—
I. In LXX.—(1) ord. sense of "adulterous," e.g. Prov. 30. 20: τοιαύτη ὁδὸς γυναικὸς μοιχαλίδος, etc.; (2) special religious sense of "unfaithful to God," derived from the idea of the relation between the Hebrew people and God as a marriage, e.g. Ezek. 23. 45: μοιχαλίδες εἰσι καὶ αἷμα ἐν χέρσιν αὐτῶν.
II. In N.T. sense (2), e.g. Matt. 12. 39: γενεὰ πονηρὰ καὶ μοιχαλὶς σημεῖον ἐπιζητεῖ; Jas. 4. 4: μοιχαλίδες οὐκ οἴδατε ὅτι ἡ φιλία τοῦ κόσμου ἐχθρὸς τοῦ θεοῦ καθίσταται (Westc.-Hort).
Late Greek degenerated to this manner of inflecting common adjectives. Cf. συγγενίς, called by Pollux, ἐσχάτως βάρβαρον; εὐγενίς, Joseph. Antiq. 7. 3. 371; ἀρχηγετίς, Inscr. Lesbos (end of third Macedonian War); καταγωγίς, CIA. ii. 2 (c. 307 B.C.).
Aristoph. the Grammarian (quoted by Lobeck) reckons among τὰ ἀσυνήθη, τὸ μοιχὴ καὶ μοιχὶς δι' ὧν δηλοῦται ἡ μοιχαλίς. μοιχαλίς is found in Plut. Placit. Phil. i. 7. 371.

σκληροτράχηλος—
I. In LXX. about six times. Always = Heb. phrase, קְשֵׁה עֹרֶף, meaning "hard of neck," i.e. obstinate. (Cf. Cic. Verr. iii. 95: tantis cervicibus est, quoted by Gesenius.)
II. In N.T. Acts 7. 51: σκληροτράχηλοι καὶ ἀπερίτμητοι καρδίαις καὶ τοῖς ὠσίν.

CONNECTION BETWEEN N.T. WORDS AND LXX. 117

σκληροτραχηλία is found in Test. Duodecim Patriarch. § 6.

ταπεινόφρων—

I. In LXX.=humble, Prov. 29. 23: τοὺς δὲ ταπεινόφρονας ἐρείδει δόξῃ κύριος.

II. In N.T. 1 Pet. 3. 8 in same sense.

Used by Plut. ii. 336 E in the sense of "low-minded."
The verb occurs in Ps. 130. 3.

Verbs

ἀναθεματίζω—

I. In LXX. always translates the Hiph'il הַחֲרִים of Heb. verb חָרַם, which has the sense of "devote to destruction." In this sense freq. in the LXX.

II. In N.T. rather in the sense of "curse," without the semi-ritual shade of meaning which it has in the LXX. Three times.

Derived from ἀνάθεμα, the parallel form to the Class. ἀνάθημα. Thus Moeris: ἀνάθημα ἀττικῶς, ἀνάθεμα ἑλληνικῶς. Similar parallels are εὕρημα in Aristoph., Plato, and Xen., and εὕρεμα in Philo, Dion. Halic., Strabo, and Galen.

Theocr. 13. 2: ἁγνῆς ἄνθεμα χρυσογόνης.

ἀποδεκατόω—

I. In LXX. (1)=pay tithes, *e.g.* Gen. 28. 22; Deut. 26. 12.

(2)=exact tithes, 1 Sam. 8. 15.

II. In N.T. (1)=(1) of LXX., Matt. 23. 23; Luke 18. 12.

(2)=(2) of LXX., Heb. 7. 5.

In the Church historian Socrates, 753 A=decimate.

βεβηλόω—

I. In LXX. a great many times in sense of "profane."

II. In N.T. twice in precisely same sense.

Occurs in Julian. Imperator, 228 C; Heliodor. 2. 25.

A noun βεβήλωσις is found in the LXX.

ἐγκαινίζω—

I. In LXX.—(1) = renew, 1 Sam. 11. 14: καὶ ἐγκαινίσωμεν ἐκεῖ τὴν βασιλείαν. So 2 Chron. 15. 8; Ps. 50. 11. (2) = consecrate, 1 Kings 8. 64: καὶ ἐνεκαίνισε τὸν οἶκον τοῦ κυρίου. So Deut. 20. 5; 2 Chron. 7. 5; Prov. 22. 6.

II. In N.T. = (2) of LXX., Heb. 9. 18, 10. 20.

Found in Eustath. *Opusc.* 277-284; Byzant. writers.

ἐξομολογέω, ἐξομολογέομαι—

I. In LXX. always middle. Direct imitation in usage of Heb. "לְ הוֹדָה = give praise to, *e.g.* 2 Sam. 22. 56: ἐξομολογήσομαί σοι κύριε ἐν τοῖς ἔθνεσιν, etc. With accus. in Ps. 88. 6: ἐξομολογήσονται οἱ οὐρανοὶ τὰ θαυμάσιά σου.

II. In N.T. usually middle = give praise, honour to; *e.g.* Matt. 11. 25: ἐξομολογοῦμαί σοι πάτερ.

Sometimes with varying shade of meaning = acknowledge joyfully, *e.g.* Apoc. 3. 5: ἐξομολογήσομαι τὸ ὄνομα αὐτοῦ, though even here the use may be exactly parallel to the last instance quoted under the LXX. In one or two places = confess.

This last sense belongs to the verb in Plut., who uses it about seven times. He has also the noun ἐξομολόγησις in the same sense, ii. 987 D, ἐξομολόγησις ἥττης. The verb also in Lucian.

ἐπιγαμβρεύω—

I. In LXX.—(1) Enter into marriage relations with, *e.g.* Gen. 34. 9: ἐπιγαμβρεύσασθαι ἡμῖν τὰς θυγατέρας ὑμῶν δότε. (2) Become son-in-law to, *e.g.* 1 Sam. 18. 22: καὶ σὺ ἐπιγάμβρευσον τῷ βασιλεῖ. Perhaps = (1). (3) Fulfil the duty of a husband's brother, Gen. 38. 8: ἐπιγάμβρευσαι αὐτήν.

II. In N.T. in sense (3) of LXX., Matt. 22. 24.

Appar. in no secular writer. Reference is made to the Schol. on Eurip. *Orest.* 574. Quite probably a colloquial word. Cf. γαμβρός in Hom., Pind., Hdt., Tragg.

ἱερατεύειν—
I. In LXX. = discharge the duties of a priest. Numerous instances.
II. In N.T. same sense, Luke 1. 8 : ἐν τῷ ἱερατεύειν αὐτόν Found nowhere before the LXX. Afterwards fairly common, e.g. Pausan. 4. 12. 6 ; Herodian, 5. 6 ; Joseph. *Antiq.* 3. 8. 1. Inscr. Mantinea (100 B.C.) : ἐπὶ ἱερέος ... Γοργίππου ... ἱερατεύσαντος. Ionic form ἱερητεύειν, found in several Inscrr. This *may* be an instance of the influence of Jewish Greek on the spoken language. For such, no doubt, there must have been. At the same time there is the other alternative, that the word was in common use in the spoken language before the LXX. was written.

πληροφορέω—
I. In LXX. = persuade fully, Eccles. 8. 11 : ἐπληροφορήθη καρδία τοῦ ποιῆσαι τὸ πονηρόν.
II. In N.T.—(1) = fulfil, e.g. Luke 1. 1 : περὶ τῶν πεπληροφορημένων ἐν ἡμῖν πραγμάτων ; 2 Tim. 4. 5 : τὴν διακονίαν σου πληροφόρησον. (2) = sense in LXX., e.g. Rom. 14. 5 : ἕκαστος ἐν τῳ ἰδίῳ νοὶ πληροφορείσθω. This reaches, in later writings, the sense of "be determined," e.g. Patriarch. 1113 C : ἐπληροφορήθην τῆς ἀναιρέσεως αὐτοῦ. Also in Byzantine writers = inform. Hence, in mod. Gk. πληροφορία = information.

None of the words given above are found earlier than the LXX., and the few which do occur outside the Bible are usually met with in the Church writers of the Christian era. Yet some of the examples, such as ἐξομολογέω, ἐπιγαμβρεύω, and ἱερατεύω, while, at first sight, they appear to be formed on the analogy of particular Hebrew words, by their sporadic currency, suggest other explanations of their existence. It is certainly possible that the LXX., giving literary form, as it did, to the spoken language of the time, may have also brought into a gradually widening currency words and senses of words previously unknown. The influence of Judæo-Greek conceptions on the Greek language of the period is an interesting subject for investigation, if there were anything like actual data on which to base it. Yet it would be hazardous to push any such hypothesis when the alternative one is so natural, viz. that words which apparently are confined to the Bible were in use in everyday life, and were adopted by the translators of the Old Testament as the nearest equivalents of the Hebrew text before them. But the majority of the terms just examined show undoubted traces of Hebrew influence, and they are only representatives of a large class.

3. The group of words common to the LXX. and New Testament which comes next in order, consists neither of religious terms nor of terms connected specially with Jewish ideas or usages. We find a large class of words denoting ordinary conceptions of everyday life which are found to have exceptional meanings in the LXX. and New Testament. Isolated instances of them appear in late authors.

The question for us is: How did they enter into the vocabulary of the New Testament? Was it through the medium of the LXX., as many scholars believe, or was it through the colloquial language of the time? The facts themselves are our only evidence. They are illustrated by the following examples:—

Nouns

ἀποστάσιον—

I. In Class. Lit. only in phrase ἀποστασίου δική = action brought against a freedman for forsaking his προστάτης, e.g. Demos. 790. 2.

II. In LXX. always translates Heb. כְּרִיתֻת = "cutting-off from marriage," i.e. divorce. Invariably in the phrase βίβλιον ἀποστασίου = bill of divorce.

III. In N.T. twice in phrase βίβλιον ἀποστασίου. Once ἀποστάσιον alone, Matt. 5. 31.

The word occurs in Simocates, a Byzantine writer (A.D. 600) = ἀπόστασις, revolt.

δῶμα—

I. In Class. Lit. = house, hall, even family.

II. In LXX. almost uniformly translates Heb. גג, meaning "roof of a house," e.g. 2 Sam. 16. 22: καὶ ἔπηξαν τὴν σκηνὴν τῷ Ἀβεσσαλὼμ ἐπὶ τὸ δῶμα.

III. In N.T. invariably = flat roof, e.g. Matt. 24. 17: ὁ δὲ ἐπὶ τοῦ δώματος μὴ καταβάτω.

In mod. Gk. δῶμα = terrace.

Jerome (*Epist. ad Suniam*) says: δῶμα in orientalibus provinciis dicitur quod apud Latinos tectum.

ἔκστασις—

I. In ordinary Greek used mainly of a condition of the mind of the nature of utter distraction caused by a shock. So freq. in Hippocrates. Combined with μεταβολή in Plut. ii. 393 D. Used by him of mental shock, i. 276 A; of love-sickness, ii. 623 C.

Aretæus (A.D. 80), an imitator of Hippocrates, defines ἔκστασις as μανία χρόνιος ἄνευθεν πυρετοῦ.

II. In LXX. it has a curious variety of uses. It translates several Hebrew words meaning respectively—(1) slander, e.g. Num. 13. 33: ἐξήνεγκαν ἔκστασιν; (2) agitation, trouble, 2 Chron. 29. 8: ἔκστασιν καὶ συρισμόν; (3) desire, wish, Ps. 30. 23: εἶπα ἐν τῇ ἐκστάσει; (4)

most freq. = terror, fear; translates two separate words, e.g. Ezek. 26. 16: ἐκστάσει ἐκστήσονται; 1 Sam. 11. 7: ἐπῆλθεν ἔκστασις κυρίου ἐπὶ τὸν λαὸν Ἰσραήλ.

The root idea in the various expressions, taking them in common, appears to be "disturbance of mind," from a strong to the weakest sense. Curiously enough, the expression ἐκστάσει διανοίας occurs in Deut. 28. 28, parallel to Plutarch's ἔκστασις τῶν λογισμῶν.

III. In N.T.—(1) technical use = "trance," e.g. Acts 10. 10: ἐγένετο ἐπ᾿ αὐτὸν ἔκστασις (the state into which Peter fell when he saw the vision regarding Cornelius). Always in connection with "visions." (2) Bewilderment, e.g. Mark 5. 42: ἐξέστησαν . . . ἐκστάσει (the feelings of the onlookers at the raising of Jairus' daughter); Acts 3. 10: ἐπλήσθησαν θάμβους καὶ ἐκστάσεως (at the healing of the lame man by Peter).

The first group of passages has a semi-technical meaning, the parent of the modern strict sense of "ecstasy." The second group has a far weaker meaning than the others, and evidently expresses simple astonishment, a considerable modification of its use in non-Biblical Greek authors.

καταστολή—

I. Fr. καταστέλλω = put in order, fit out, e.g. Eurip. Bacch. 933: πλόκαμον. But chiefly = restrain, e.g. Epictet. Diss. 3. 19. 5: τὴν ἐπιθυμίαν; Plut. ii. 207 E: τοὺς νέους. The noun in non-Biblical writers usu. = quietness in appearance, attire, e.g. Plut. Pericl. 5: καταστολὴ τῆς περιβολῆς.

II. In LXX. Isa. 61. 3: καταστολὴν δόξης ἀντὶ πνεύματος ἀκηδίας, where it translates Heb. מַעֲטֶה, meaning veil or garment.

III. In N.T. 1 Tim. 2. 9: γυναῖκας ἐν καταστολῇ κοσμίῳ, where the context and the epithet seem to demand the meaning "dress," "attire." Plut. ii. 65 D has the verb καταστολίζω = vestire.

Hesych.: καταστολήν· περιβολήν. Undoubtedly a number

of instances are cited from Hippocrates, where it seems to mean "modesty in appearance." Ellicott holds there is no authority for the meaning "dress," and calls it "deportment as exhibited externally, whether in look, manner, or dress." But the evidence already cited seems to us ample.

νύμφη—
I. In Class. Lit. = bride, young wife, or marriageable girl. Then = nymph.
II. In LXX. out of thirty-four passages, in thirty-three it translates Heb. כַּלָּה, which means—(1) bride; (2) daughter-in-law, in which sense alone it is found in Gen. 11. 31, 38. 11; Lev. 18. 15, 20. 12; Ruth 1. 6, 2. 20, 4. 15; 1 Kings 4. 20; 1 Chron. 2. 4.
III. In N.T. = daughter-in-law, Luke 12. 53: πενθερὰ ἐπὶ τὴν νύμφην καὶ νύμφη ἐπὶ τὴν πενθεράν. So in Matt. Cf. Joseph. Antiq. 5. 9. 1: οὐκ ἐκαρτέρουν δὲ διαζευγνύμεναι αὐτῆς αἱ νύμφαι.

ὀχύρωμα—
I. In Class. Lit. = fortress, Xen.
II. In LXX.—(1) very often = fortress; (2) metaph. use = that in which confidence is placed, e.g. Prov. 10. 29: ὀχύρωμα ὁσίον φόβος κυρίου; Prov. 21. 22: καθεῖλεν τὸ ὀχύρωμα ἐφ' ᾧ ἐπεπόνθεσαν οἱ ἀσεβεῖς.
III. In N.T. last sense, 2 Cor. 10. 4: δυνατὰ . . . πρὸς καθαίρεσιν ὀχυρωμάτων.
Cf. Philo, de Abrah. 38: τὸν ἐπιτειχισμὸν τῶν ἐναντίων δοξῶν καθαιρεῖν (Alford).

πρόσωπον—
I. In Class. Lit. = face, front, mask, character, person.
II. In LXX.—(1) ordinary senses of "face"; (2) metaph. sense, Gen. 2. 6: ἐπότιζε πᾶν τὸ πρόσωπον τῆς γῆς; Ps. 104. 30: ἀνακαινιεῖς τὸ πρόσωπον τῆς γῆς.
III. In N.T.—(1) ordinary meanings; (2) special sense as above = outward appearance, "*species externa*";

Luke 12. 56: τὸ πρόσωπον τῆς γῆς καὶ τοῦ οὐρανοῦ;
Jas. 1. 11: ἡ εὐπρέπεια τοῦ προσώπου αὐτοῦ ἀπώλετο.

ῥῆμα—
I. In Class. Lit. = (1) word; (2) phrase.
II. In LXX. in overwhelming majority of cases = Hebrew
דָּבָר, meaning (1) word, but in these places (2) thing,
occurrence.
III. In N.T.—(1) Ordinary meaning in all its varieties;
(2) sense as in LXX. Luke 1. 37: οὐκ ἀδυνατήσει παρὰ
τῷ θεῷ πᾶν ῥῆμα; Acts 10. 37: τὸ γενόμενον ῥῆμα;
5. 32: ἡμεῖς ἐσμὲν μάρτυρες τῶν ῥημάτων τούτων. In all
these places ῥῆμα = occurrence. A suggestion of this
usage found in the semi-parallel use of λόγος, e.g. Soph.
Aj. 1288: εἰ σοῦ γ' ὅδ' ἀνὴρ οὐδ' ἐπὶ σμικρῶν λόγων . . .
ἔτ' ἴσχει μνῆστιν, where λόγος seems quite colourless.
Also in Plato, e.g. in *Phil*. 33 C: ἐὰν πρὸς λόγον ᾖ,
where λόγος = the matter in hand.

Verbs

ἀδυνατέω—
I. In Class. Lit. in Plato and Aristot. = want strength, be
unable to do anything.
II. In LXX. = be impossible, e.g. Job 42. 2: πάντα δύνασαι,
ἀδυνατεῖ δὲ σοι οὐδέν; Zech. 8. 6: εἰ ἀδυνατήσει ἐνώπιον
τῶν καταλοίπων μὴ ἐνώπιόν μου ἀδυνατήσει.
III. Twice in N.T. Same sense, Matt. 17. 20: ἐρεῖτε τῷ
ὄρει τούτῳ· μετάβα ἔνθεν ἐκεῖ καὶ μεταβήσεται καὶ οὐδὲν
ἀδυνατήσει ὑμῖν; Luke 1. 37: οὐκ ἀδυνατήσει παρὰ
τοῦ θεοῦ πᾶν ῥῆμα (v.l. παρὰ τῷ θεῷ). Cf. Polyb. 16.
33. 3: ὅτε τι τούτων ἀχρειωθὲν ἀδυνατήσειε. The word
is extraordinarily common in Philo, and yet apparently
always in the ordinary sense.

ἀποκρίνω—
I. In Class. Lit.—(1) distinguish, separate; (2) middle =
answer. (A few other subordinate senses.)
II. In the LXX. in a vast majority of instances it translates

CONNECTION BETWEEN N.T. WORDS AND LXX. 125

Heb. עָנָה, which is constantly used in the sense of "beginning to speak," *i.e.* "taking up the conversation."

III. In N.T. — (1) answer (usually with passive forms); (2) over a dozen instances of the peculiar usage already mentioned when the verb is used of a person *beginning to speak*, and not answering any question, but at the same time referring to something that has gone before, *e.g.* Matt. 17. 4 : ἀποκριθεὶς δὲ ὁ Πέτρος εἶπεν τῷ Ἰησοῦ (with reference to the scene on the mountain of transfiguration). Bengel says : "Respondit non modo qui rogatus est sed cui causa loquendi est data."

κρίνω—

I. In Class. Lit.—(1) pick out; (2) decide; (3) judge or estimate ; (4) accuse; (5) condemn.

II. In LXX. a number of passages in Judges, where κρίνειν τὸν λαόν is used in the sense of "govern." Constantly in this sense throughout the O.T., *e.g.* 2 Kings 15. 5 : καὶ υἱὸς τοῦ βασιλέως ἐπὶ τῷ οἴκῳ κρίνων τὸν λαὸν τῆς γῆς; Ps. 2. 10 : καὶ νῦν βασιλεῖς σύνετε· παιδεύθητε πάντες οἱ κρίνοντες τὴν γῆν, etc. etc. It translates the Heb. שָׁפַט, which has this sense constantly; cf. "suffetes" (same word) for chief rulers of Carthage. Cf. Sap. Salom. i. 1 : ἀγαπήσατε δικαιοσύνην οἱ κρίνοντες τὴν γῆν, on which Grimm says : "The special term κρίνειν, instead of the more general κυριεύειν or βασιλεύειν, according to the Hebrew usage, because in the East the pronouncing of judgment was a chief function of the ruler."

III. In N.T. the ordinary senses of "estimate," "judge," "decide," "condemn," as in Class. Greek. But in several places it follows the sense noted under the LXX., *e.g.* Matt. 19. 28 : ὅταν καθίσῃ ὁ υἱὸς τοῦ ἀνθρώπου ἐπὶ θρόνον δόξης αὐτοῦ, καθίσεσθε καὶ αὐτοὶ ἐπὶ δώδεκα θρόνους κρίνοντες τοὺς δώδεκα φυλὰς τοῦ Ἰσραήλ ; 1 Cor. 6. 3 : οὐκ οἴδατε ὅτι ἀγγέλους κρινοῦμεν ; cf. Artemid. ii. 12. 56 : κρίνειν γὰρ τὸ ἄρχειν ἔλεγον οἱ παλαιοί; Joseph. *Antt.* 5. 3. 1 : λαμβάνει παρὰ τοῦ πλήθους ἀρχὴν ὥστε κρίνειν τὸν λαόν.

θροέω—

I. In Class. Lit.—(1) cry aloud, Aesch., Soph.; (2) utter aloud, Aesch., Soph., Eur.

II. In LXX. used to translate Hebrew הָמָה = be disquieted in mind, Cant. 5. 4: καὶ ἡ κοιλία μου ἐθροήθη ἐπ' αὐτόν.

III. In N.T. same sense, Matt. 24. 6: ὁρᾶτε μὴ θροεῖσθε; Mark 13. 7: ὅταν δὲ ἀκούσητε πολέμους καὶ ἀκοὰς πολέμων μὴ θροεῖσθε; 2 Thess. 2. 2: εἰς τὸ μὴ ταχέως σαλευθῆναι ὑμᾶς ἀπὸ τοῦ νοὸς μηδὲ θροεῖσθαι. Cf. an epigram quoted by Jacobs: αὐτὴ τεκοῦσα παρθένος πάλιν μένει, καὶ μὴ θροηθῇς ἔστι γὰρ τὸ παιδίον θεός, where, according to Lobeck, μὴ θροηθῇς = μὴ θαυμάσῃς.

λικμάω—

I. In Class. Lit. = winnow, Hom. Xen.

II. In LXX.—(1) Winnow, three or four instances. (2) Scatter, e.g. 1 Kings 14. 15: καὶ λικμήσει αὐτοὺς ἀπὸ πέραν τοῦ ποταμοῦ; Ezek. 29. 12: λικμήσω αὐτοὺς εἰς τὰς χώρας; Job 27. 21: λικμήσει αὐτὸν ἐκ τοῦ τόπου αὐτοῦ (in this passage a different Heb. word = hurl out of sight). (3) Dan. 2. 44: (Theodot.): λεπτυνεῖ καὶ λικμήσει πάσας τὰς βασιλείας καὶ αὐτὴ ἀναστήσεται εἰς τοὺς αἰῶνας, where λικμάω translates a Chaldean word = make an end of. The LXX. translates here ἀφανίσει.

III. In N.T. Matt. 21. 44: ἐφ' ὃν δ' ἂν πέσῃ [ὁ λίθος] λικμήσει αὐτόν (omitted by Tischendorf; Westcott-Hort and Lachmann bracket it); Luke 20. 18: πᾶς ὁ πεσὼν ἐπ' ἐκεῖνον τὸν λίθον συνθλασθήσεται· ἐφ' ὃν δ' ἂν πέσῃ λικμήσει αὐτόν; Sir John Cheke transl.: "It will drive him like dust awai." The sense of A.V., "grind to powder," is exaggerated. "Scattering" is the ruling notion, as in the LXX. Carr (on Luke 20. 18) suggests that the idea comes from a mode of winnowing common in Egypt, in which a "tribulum" was drawn over the corn by which the grain was separated and the straw broken, after which the corn was again winnowed with a fork. Thus the notion of breaking and crushing is

CONNECTION BETWEEN N.T. WORDS AND LXX. 127

clearly associated with winnowing, and that in the neighbourhood of Alexandria.

μωραίνω—

I. In Class. Lit. = play the fool, Aesch., Eur., Xen. In Pass. = be stupefied, Aristot.

II. In LXX. = make foolish, e.g. Isa. 19. 11: οἱ σοφοὶ σύμβουλοι, ἡ βουλὴ αὐτῶν μωρανθήσεται; Jer. 10. 13: ἐμωράνθη πᾶς ἄνθρωπος ἀπὸ γνώσεως; Isa. 44. 25: τὴν βουλὴν αὐτῶν μωραίνων.

III. In N.T.—(1) = sense in LXX. Rom. 1. 22: φάσκοντες εἶναι σοφοὶ ἐμωράνθησαν; 1 Cor. 1. 20: ἐμώρανεν ὁ θεὸς τὴν σοφίαν. (2) Make tasteless, insipid; Matt. 5. 13: ἐὰν δὲ . . . τὸ ἅλας μωρανθῇ, ἐν τίνι ἀρτυθήσεται; For interchange of meaning between folly and insipidity, the commentators compare "sapere," "sapientia," "insipidus." Sal, sales = wit. Late Greek, ἅλες. "Insulsus" = stupid. Cf. Dioscor. (quoted by Wetstein): ῥίζαι γευσαμένῳ μωραί.

πατάσσω—

I. In Class. Lit. = beat, or smite, Hom., Tragg., Oratt., Plato. In Demos. Aristocr. 645: ἐὰν λίθος ἢ ξύλον ἢ σίδηρος ἤ τι τοιοῦτον ἐμπεσὸν πατάξῃ . . . αὐτὸ δ᾽ εἰδῇ . . . τὸ τὸν φόνον εἰργασμένον, it means apparently "kill."

II. In LXX. almost always translates Heb. הִכָּה (Hiph'il of נָכָה not used) = "smite," but especially in the following two senses—(1) Kill, e.g. Ex. 2. 12: καὶ πατάξας τὸν Αἰγύπτιον, ἔκρυψεν αὐτόν; Judg. 3. 31: καὶ ἐπάταξεν τοὺς ἀλλοφύλους εἰς ἑξακοσίους ἄνδρας. So constantly. (2) Visit with evil (sickness, calamity, etc.), e.g. Deut. 28. 22: πατάξαι σε κύριος ἐν ἀπορίᾳ καὶ πυρέτῳ; Isa. 14. 6: πατάξας ἔθνος πληγῇ ἀνιάτῳ.

III. In N.T.—(1) Ordinary sense = smite. (2) Kill, Matt. 26. 31: πατάξω τὸν ποιμένα καὶ διασκορπισθήσονται τὰ πρόβατα (qn. fr. LXX.); Acts 7. 24. (3) = (2) under the LXX. Apoc. 11. 6: ἐξουσίαν ἔχουσιν . . . πατάξαι τὴν γῆν ἐν πάσῃ πληγῇ; Acts 12. 33: παραχρῆμα δὲ ἐπάταξεν αὐτὸν ἄγγελος κυρίου.

συνάγω—
I. In Class. Lit. = "bring together," in every possible sense.
II. In LXX. in the sense of "entertain," but almost always with εἰς οἶκον and the like, e.g. Judg. 19. 15 : καὶ οὐκ ἔστιν ἀνὴρ ὁ συνάγων αὐτοὺς εἰς τὸν οἶκον; 2 Sam. 11. 29 : συνήγαγεν αὐτὴν εἰς τὸν οἶκον αὐτοῦ; Gen. 29. 22 : συνήγαγεν δὲ Λαβὰν πάντας τοὺς ἄνδρας τοῦ τόπου καὶ ἐποίησεν γάμον. Also the curious phrase in 2 Kings 5. 3: τότε ἀποσυνάξει αὐτὸν ἀπὸ τῆς λέπρας αὐτοῦ = receive a leper into intercourse, i.e. when cured. ἀποσυνάξει translates the same word as in the other instances.
III. In N.T. (1) ordinary sense common; (2) entertain, Matt. 25. 35 : ξένος ἤμην καὶ συνηγάγετέ με, etc.
This word marks colloquial growth. The addition εἰς τὸν οἶκον (LXX.) gradually fell away.
Cf. Plut. Symp. ii. 10, p. 643: ἑστιάτωρ ἀνθρώπους οὔτε διψῶντας ὡσαύτως οὔτε πεινῶντας εἰς ταὐτὸ συναγαγών; Plut. ii. 1097 E: συνάγειν ἑστίασιν; Strabo, 14, p. 948: συνάγειν συμπόσια. Weiss refers to Xen. Cyr. 5. 3. 11 for the same signification. Perhaps the beginnings of the usage are seen in expressions like συνάγειν ξυσσίτια in Plato, etc. Possibly also συνάγειν ἀπὸ συμβολῶν = have a picnic, Diphil. Ζωγρ. 2. 28.

One or two subordinate groups of words remain yet to be noticed in this section.

4. A certain class of words occurs both in the LXX. and the New Testament, which scholars have been accustomed to call "Alexandrian." These have no immediate connection with Hebrew influences, and they are certainly almost unknown outside the sphere of Biblical Greek. It might seem, therefore, a legitimate assumption that their appearance in the New Testament is due to the

influence of the LXX. Still, there are stray evidences from one quarter or another which make it highly probable that they formed part of the popular speech of the time, and which afford us an additional reason for ceasing to speak of an "Alexandrian" dialect,—a custom apparently due to the need of some convenient phrase for covering a group of facts regarding which our data are extremely meagre. The following are typical instances, and serve to show how far we are entitled to make inferences from the actual facts:—

ἀλίσγημα—

This noun occurs in the N.T. Acts 15. 20: ἀπέχεσθαι τῶν ἀλισγημάτων τῶν εἰδώλων (in speech of St. James). The same idea is expressed in ver. 29 by εἰδωλοθύτων. Hesych. on the word says: 'Αλισγημάτων· τῆς μεταλήψεως τῶν μωρῶν θυσιῶν.

The verb ἀλισγέω occurs only in the LXX. Dan. 1. 8 (Theodot.): ὅπως μὴ ἀλισγηθῇ ἐν τῷ δείπνῳ τοῦ βασιλέως; Mal. 1. 7: ἄρτους ἠλισγημένους; ver. 12: τράπεζα κυρίου ἠλισγημένη ἐστι. In all these places it translates Heb. Pual Ptcp. of גָּאַל = pollute.

So Hesych.: ἀλισγοῦντες· μολύνοντες, μιαίνοντες. A Schol. on Mal. 1. 7, explains by μεμολυσμένους.

ἀμφιάζω—

I. In LXX. Job 29. 14: δικαιοσύνην δὲ ἐνδεδύκειν, ἠμφιασάμην δὲ κρίμα ἴσα διπλοΐδι; Job 40. 5: ἀνάλαβε δὴ ὕψος καὶ δύναμιν, δόξαν δὲ καὶ τιμὴν ἀμφίασαι. (So א A.)

II. In N.T. Luke 12. 28: εἰ δὲ . . . τὸν χόρτον . . . ὁ θεὸς οὕτως ἀμφιάζει. (So Lachm., Westc.-Hort.)

τὸ μὲν ἀμφιέζω ἐστὶ κοινῶς, τὸ δὲ ἀμφιάζω Δωρικόν, ὥσπερ τὸ ὑποπιέζω καὶ ὑποπιάζω, Cram. *Anecdot. Oxon.* ii. 338. 31 (quoted by Grimm). The verb occurs in Diod. 16. 11; Plut. ii. 120 B; *Anthol.* iii. 12; Inscrr. Noun ἀμφίασις in Job 22. 6, 38. 9; ἀμφίασμα, Luc. *Cyn.* 17;

ἀπαμφιάζω, Plut. ii. 406 D ; Philo, several times. Cf. ποία = ποίη.

ἀποκεφαλίζω—
I. In LXX. Ps. 151. 7 : ἀπεκεφάλισα αὐτόν (David and Goliath).
II. In N.T. Matt. 14. 10 : καὶ πέμψας ἀπεκεφάλισεν Ἰωάννην ἐν τῇ φυλακῇ. So Mark 6. 16; Luke 9. 10 (always in the story of the Baptist).
Cf. Dion Cass. 71. 28 : ὥστε ἀποκεφαλισθέντος οὐδὲ τὴν κεφαλὴν αὐτοῦ ἰδεῖν ὑπέμεινεν; Arrian, Artem. Oneiroc. 1. 35. Lobeck says it is never found in Attic, and compares "*decollare*" in Plautus.
Plut. *de Is. et Osir.* uses ἀποκεφαλισμός. Strabo, 531, has ἀποκεφαλιστής.

ἐμπαιγμός—
= Mockery. LXX. and N.T. Apparently no instances in Attic of ἐμπαίζω in the sense of "mock" = προσπαίζω or καταπαίζω. Once in this sense in Herodotus. As Rutherford observes, it might be expected that this sense would present itself on the analogy of Latin "*illudo*." "ἐμπαικτής, ἔμπαιγμα, ἐμπαιγμός, Alexandrina aetas protulit" (Lobeck).

ἐνωτίζομαι—
I. In LXX. exceedingly often (about thirty times) = give ear to, Gen. 4. 23, etc. etc. Usually translates Heb. הֶאֱזִין, derived from the Hebrew noun אֹזֶן = "ear."
II. In N.T. only Acts 2. 14. Sturz considers Vorst to have proved that the word was in existence in the "vulgar" speech before the LXX. Stier quotes a parallel Latin form, "*inaurire*," from Lactantius. Often in later writers, such as Gregory Nazianzen and Zonaras.

ἐξολεθρεύω (or ἐξολοθρεύω)—
I. In LXX. an innumerable number of times, to translate about seven different Hebrew words = destroy, kill.

CONNECTION BETWEEN N.T. WORDS AND LXX. 131

II. In N.T. only in Acts.
Schol. Aristoph. Plut. 443: ἐξολοθρευτικώτερον; Joseph. *Antiq.* 8. 4. 280: καὶ πᾶν ἐξολοθρεύσω σου τὸ γένος. (But Niese reads ἐξολέσω.) Plut. i. 965 E. Often in Testament of the Twelve Patriarchs. The noun ἐξολέθρευσις in Josephus.
Form ὀλο(ε)θρεύειν. Philo, *Leg. Alleg.* ii. 9. 1: ἐᾷ τὸν ὀλοθρεύοντα εἰσελθεῖν; *Etym. Mag.*: ὀλλύειν ὅ ἐστιν ὀλοθρεύειν. So also Schol. Eurip. Hippol. 535; *Anthol. Pal.* i. 57; Suidas: ὀλέσκει· ὀλοθρεύει; Krebs (quoted by Sturz): "vox est mere Alexandrina."

ἐξυπνίζω—
I. In LXX., *e.g.* 1 Kings 3. 15: καὶ ἐξυπνίσθη Σολομών; Judg. 16. 13: ἐξυπνίσθη ἐκ τοῦ ὕπνου.
II. In N.T. John 11. 12: πορεύομαι ἵνα ἐξυπνίσω αὐτόν. Condemned by the Grammarians Phrynichus, Moeris, Herodian, Thomas.
E.g. Phryn. 200: ἐξυπνισθῆναι οὐ χρὴ λέγειν ἀλλ' ἀφυπνισθῆναι. Found in Plut. ii. 979 C; M. Antonin. 6. 31: καὶ ἐξυπνισθεὶς πάλιν καὶ ἐννοήσας ὅτι ὄνειροί σοι ἠνώχλουν. Often in Church writers and the Testament of the Twelve Patriarchs. ἔξυπνος in Joseph. *Antiq.* 11. 3. 2; M. Antonin. 10. 13.

εὐδοκία—
I. In LXX., *e.g.* Ps. 18. 15: καὶ ἔσονται εἰς εὐδοκίαν τὰ λόγια τοῦ στόματός μου; and elsewhere, especially in Psalms.
II. In N.T. repeatedly, *e.g.* Luke 10. 21: οὕτως ἐγένετο εὐδοκία ἔμπροσθέν σου. Usually = goodwill. Rom. 10. 1: ἡ εὐδοκία τῆς ἐμῆς καρδίας = eager desire. The verb εὐδοκέω (often in LXX. and N.T.) is exceptionally common in Polybius and Diodorus. It was evidently a "common" word.

ἱεράτευμα—
= ἱερεῖς. I. In LXX. Repeatedly in this sense in the Pentateuch.

II. In N.T. 1 Pet. 2. 5, same sense. Sturz quotes it as an instance of an Attic formation which finds place in Alexandrian Greek, the abstract for the concrete. So ἐξουθένημα for ἐξουθενηθείς in Ps. 21. 6. Parallel to places like Plato, *Timæ.* iii. 24 D : παίδευμα = παιδευθείς.

μεγαλειότης—

Several times in LXX. and N.T. = majesty.

Plutarch is quoted by Lobeck as pointing out that Chrysippus brought in many unwonted words into philosophy, as χαριεντότης, καλότης, μεγαλότης, etc. A great mass of words of this formation is said to be found in the Scholiasts belonging to this time. The word occurs in *Athenæ.* 4. 6. 130. The adj. is found in Xen., Joseph., Polyb.

5. The last important subdivision of words which it is possible to regard as having passed into the vocabulary of the New Testament through the influence of the LXX. is that which may be briefly designated as *New Compound Words.* A large number of these appear only in the LXX. and New Testament. But it has been already noted more than once that this is one of the most characteristic phenomena of the later language. So that we need not be astonished at finding a special group of "Compounds" peculiar to the Biblical writers. It is only surprising that this is not wider in range than it is, seeing that the Biblical writings are the only monuments of the spoken language, strictly so called, which we possess.

The following are instances of this class :—

Nouns—

ἀπαύγασμα, ἐγκαίνια, ἐμπαικτής, ἥττημα, κατάνυξις, κατοικητήριον, καύχησις, μεγαλωσύνη, μετοικεσία, ὁρκωμοσία,

CONNECTION BETWEEN N.T. WORDS AND LXX. 133

παραπικρασμός, πεποίθησις, πρωτοτοκία, ὑπακοή, ὑπολήνιον, ὑστέρημα, ψευδοπροφήτης.

Adjectives—
ἀκατάσχετος, ἀκρογωνιαῖος, ἀλλογένης, ἀνεξιχνίαστος, ἀπερίτμητος, δυσβάστακτός, ἐπικατάρατος, μογίλαλος, νεόφυτος, ὀλιγόψυχος, πρωτότοκος, σητόβρωτος.

Verbs—
ἀγαθοποιέω, ἀναζώννυμι, ἀποφθέγγομαι, ἀνταποκρίνομαι, διαγογγύζω, ἐκζητέω, ἐκμυκτηρίζω, ἐκπειράζω, ἐκπορνεύω, ἐκριζόω, ἐμπεριπατέω, ἐνδιδύσκω, ἐνδοξάζω, ἐνευλογέω, ἐνταφιάζω, ἐξαστράπτω, ἐξουδενέω, ἐπαναπαύω, ἐπιφαύσκω, κατακαυχάομαι, κατακληρονομέω, κατανύσσω, κλυδωνίζομαι, κραταιόω, ὀρθοτομέω, παραζηλόω, συνεγείρω, σκανδαλίζω, ὑποστρώννυμι.

CHAPTER X

DISCUSSION OF THE GENERAL QUESTION OF THE INFLUENCE OF THE LXX. ON THE VOCABULARY OF THE NEW TESTAMENT, BASED ON THE RESULTS REACHED

AFTER the inquiries concluded in last section, it ought to be possible to give some more or less definite answer to the question: What is the influence of the Septuagint on the vocabulary of the New Testament?

A few statistics must be recalled.

1. An overwhelming majority of the words which make up the vocabulary of the New Testament is pre-Aristotelian. In fact, 80 per cent. of the whole number dates from before 322 B.C.

(*a*) A great part of these consists of words which denote concrete ideas.

a. Many of them naturally bear the same meaning in the New Testament as they do throughout the whole course of Greek literature.

β. A certain number, however, show peculiar significations in the New Testament which are paralleled by similar uses in the LXX. But from constant traces of cognate meanings in contemporary writers, and those, in particular, as they approach the common vernacular, we are only entitled to say that the special meanings are due to and derived from the ordinary spoken language of the time.

(b) This portion of the New Testament language also includes a large number of words which are designations of abstract ideas.

a. Of these, a great many, just as in the former class, either have the same significations in the New Testament as in other Greek books of all periods, or show the influence of the colloquial language of the day by various modifications of their original usage, and diverging shades of meaning belonging to a late date in the history of the Greek tongue.

β. There is another group of terms, however, which falls under this heading, and which has been already designated as "religious and theological." The words which express them are, in great measure, ordinary Greek words, but many of these, at least, have been adapted to this use by the translators of the Old Testament. Accordingly, these words have had a special colour imparted to them by the Hebrew content with which they have been filled, although it must be said that they, in particular, have been chosen because they offered easy points of junction for the new meanings which they were destined to have. And so they form a sort of theological terminology which has naturally become a model for the New Testament writers. Yet it must be borne in mind that while we have in the New Testament over three hundred words altogether which have a special "Biblical" meaning, only about one hundred of these occur with a similar sense in the LXX., *i.e.* about 35 per cent. of the whole.

2. The remaining portion of the New Testament vocabulary consists of about nine hundred and fifty words which are not found in any author previous to the death of Aristotle. Of these, about five hundred and fifty, roughly speaking, are " Biblical," *i.e.* found either in the New Testament alone, or, besides, only in the LXX. To go a step farther, nearly four hundred of the last-mentioned group are absolutely peculiar to the New Testament, leaving about one hundred and sixty common to the New Testament and LXX., and found in no other place. We have already given a pretty full analysis of these one hundred and sixty words, showing that a number of them are probably formations by the writers of the LXX. on the model of Hebrew terms, or, at least, distinct adaptations of Greek forms to express Semitic conceptions; while the rest are either late words, in whose case it is merely an accident of history that they are only found in Biblical writers, or special phenomena of the popular dialect with perhaps a certain amount of local colouring.

The influence of the Septuagint on the New Testament vocabulary has often been, and is still, absurdly exaggerated. It is no wonder that misconceptions in regard to this matter prevail, when a scholar like the late Dr. Hatch goes the length of saying:[1] "The *great majority* of New Testament words are words which, though for the most part common to Biblical and to contemporary secular Greek, express in their Biblical use the conceptions of a Semitic race, and which must consequently be examined by the light of the cognate

[1] *Essays in Biblical Greek*, p. 34. The italics are ours.

documents which form the LXX." This is simply *not* the case. Assuredly, the documents which form the LXX. shed valuable light on the language of the New Testament. But why? Because they are the only other records we possess of the current popular speech prevailing at the time. Dr. Hatch compares the use of Greek by the Jews to that of English by a Hindoo Mussulman. Surely this is an extraordinarily misleading comparison, especially as regards the Jews of New Testament times. It would be nearer the mark if he had told us that the Hindoo's great-grandfather had settled in England, and that his descendants, with the exception of some stray visits to their ancestral country, resided in the British Islands, and had become naturalised English citizens.

Again he says [1] (and this in reference to vocabulary): "Biblical Greek is a language which stands by itself." For parts of the LXX., no doubt, this is true. But that is because it is a slavishly literal translation, and it was necessary either to force ordinary Greek words to bear a sense which was not natural to them, or else coin new words on the analogy of Hebrew. For the New Testament it is *not* true, except as regards that one group of theological terms which are naturally modelled on the similar terminology of the LXX., but which, after all, far overpass their Old Testament bounds, and also the small group of words expressing rites and customs and special conceptions of the Jews which had passed over bodily from the LXX.

Dr. Hatch lays down a Canon for the study of the

[1] *Essays*, p. 11.

LXX., with special reference to its use in determining the meaning of New Testament words.[1] "A word which is used uniformly, or with few and intelligible exceptions, as the translation of the same Hebrew word, must be held to have in Biblical Greek the same meaning as that Hebrew word." This, of course, is meant to apply strictly to the New Testament vocabulary. We admit this absolutely in the group of New Testament words which are the direct outgrowth of Hebrew theology, as δόξα, διάβολος, εἰρήνη, πειράζω, and the like. We also admit it with restrictions in the case of terms denoting Jewish usages, which were presumably formed by the writers of the LXX., but which, by New Testament times, seem to have become more lax in their use, and in a few cases to have passed into the ordinary vocabulary of the period. Hence, accordingly, they underwent various modifications in their meaning. But in reference to the vocabulary of Biblical Greek, as a whole, it appears to us quite untenable for many reasons.

To begin with, it is admitted on all hands that the translators of the LXX. were exceedingly unskilful workmen. Some of them show far greater stupidity than others. Suppose, then, a case which constantly occurs, that of a word only found, though very often found, in a book which betrays great inaccuracy. The same Greek word is always used to translate one Hebrew word. It is used in a very exceptional sense, quite alien to its ordinary meaning. And the reason is that the translator has no proper grasp of Greek, or else, from

[1] *Essays*, p. 35.

an imperfect knowledge of Hebrew, he mixes up two significations, and so uses a word inaccurately. This same Greek word occurs in the New Testament. Are we to make its use in the LXX. our criterion of its meaning there? We may have abundance of contemporary evidence for its usage; we may know the special characteristics of the writer in whom it is found. Surely these are safer tests to apply than that which Dr. Hatch lays down.

Another consideration, in this regard, is important. We have a great mass of evidence to show that the translators of the LXX. had a tendency to use a Greek word which was the equivalent for the ordinary signification of a Hebrew word, in its secondary senses as well.[1] But this is no criterion of usage. It is often the result of mere individual predilection, and yet it may fall exactly under Dr. Hatch's Canon. Surely it would be very unsafe to allow this to regulate our determination of the New Testament vocabulary.

But, further, there is the question of time. Several hundreds of years have elapsed between the two collections of writings. In proportion as the Jews have mingled with other nations, and often come to regard Greek as their native tongue, words which originally had a close connection with Semitic conceptions must necessarily have tended to approach nearer to contemporary Greek usage, and may appear even to

---

[1] *E.g.* ὀφείλημα = (1) debt; (2) sin.
χεῖλος = (1) lip; (2) language.
ἐρωτᾶν = (1) interrogate; (2) request.
δικαιοσύνη = (1) righteousness; (2) alms. Cf. Winer (Eng. trans.), p. 33 sq.

have become part of the literary vocabulary of the time.

Besides, as we have tried to show in discussing the vocabulary of the New Testament, the writers of the books belonging to it manifest a far truer grasp of the Greek language, and even a certain literary tone, in the words they use. So that, except in the case of technical and theological terms, they move on a higher level than the translators of the LXX.

One further consideration must be specified, and that a very important one. The LXX. is essentially a translation, and that from a language whose genius is alien to that of Greek. Also, it is extraordinarily literal. This being so, are we at liberty to make its phenomena absolute standards of usage? The very peculiarities in its use of words, and the meanings it gives to them, are due to nothing else than the sheer literalness of the translation. It is hard to see how this can, except in cases which are quite obvious, stamp a word for all time coming with a particular sense. Indeed, many of these particular senses are thoroughly isolated, and could not, on any consideration, lead us to expect their repetition in the language of the New Testament, which is the spontaneous expression of vivid conceptions, born in the minds of men, most of whom have a thorough acquaintance with the colloquial language of their day, and can exercise themselves in it freely.

The fact is, when we consider the place the LXX. must have occupied among the Jewish people both in Palestine and the adjacent countries, as testified by the New Testament itself, we may well be astonished to find that its influence has been, comparatively speaking, so small. If we take, for instance, the 103rd Psalm, which must have been thoroughly well known to all Jews, we find within its narrow compass words such as δεσπόζω, δυνάστεια, ἐξανθέω, εὐιλατεύω, μακρόθυμος, μακρύνω, μηνίω, πολυέλεος, all of them terms which might easily have found a place in the New Testament vocabulary, but which do not occur there.

Professor Abbott gives some striking instances of the marked differences which exist between the two vocabularies.[1] Thus the verb βαστάζω, which occurs twenty-seven times in the New Testament, is only found once in the LXX. The group βαρέω, βέβαιος, βραδύς, βραδύνω, βραδύτης, all appearing in the New Testament, are not in the LXX.

Differences in the significations of words are well exemplified by the noun ἀγάπη, which in the LXX. is used of love as between the sexes, and which, on the contrary, appears in the New Testament of that high spiritual love which finds its chief object in God, in other words, love without passion. The term which expresses this conception in the LXX. is ἀγάπησις, never found in the New Testament. So also ὑπομονή in the LXX.= expectation, in the New Testament = patient endurance. ἄφεσις in LXX.= dismissal, in New Testament = remission of sins, a conception expressed in the LXX. by ἱλασμός.

Again, Abbott points out that often in reference to

[1] *Essays on the Original Texts of the Old and New Testaments*, p. 70 sq.

ideas where we should expect the LXX. to influence the New Testament, there are great divergences—

> *E.g.* " Confess " = ἐξαγορεύω in LXX.
>   ,,   = ἐξομολογέομαι in N.T.,
>   which = "praise" in LXX.
> " Divorce " = ἐξαποστέλλειν in LXX.
>   ,,   = ἀπολύειν in N.T. etc. etc.

This list might be indefinitely extended.

Let us apply now, by way of summary, the various possibilities of relationship between any two vocabularies, which were laid down on pp. 87, 88, to the case of the LXX. and New Testament.

(1.) The first holds strictly in the present instance. There is no doubt whatever that the LXX. is thoroughly well known to the writers of the New Testament, and it is unnecessary to dwell upon this after what has been already said.

(2.) The second may be also considered to be verified. It is the fact that an overwhelmingly large proportion of the vocabulary of the New Testament has already occurred in the LXX. But this is subject to most important restrictions. By far the greater part of the common stock of words is found in Greek writers of all periods. And the group which comes easily next, numerically, consists partly of late words and forms in general, partly of colloquial words which have found little or no place in literature, except in the Biblical writings.

(3.) The third possibility cannot be said to be true in the case before us. Considering the intimate acquaintance with the LXX. which the New Testament writers reveal, it is surprising to find how small a number of the words appearing in the New Testament occur in no other known writings except the LXX.

It is extremely probable that the list of special "Biblical" words which does exist will be diminished from year to year by fresh discoveries of inscriptions and "finds" of new manuscripts which (like the Mimes of Herondas) may be of a kind fitted to shed light on the popular language. The works of many of the later writers, too, have not, as yet, been examined with sufficient care and accuracy, so that in the case, for example, of Josephus and many more, it is impossible to estimate their vocabularies with anything like precision. In any case, it is not going too far to say that those advances which may be made in knowledge of the current colloquial language, are certain to make the list we are examining, small though it be, considerably less. A striking instance of this process may be seen by comparing Professor Thayer's careful list of "words peculiar to the LXX. and New Testament," drawn up in 1888, with the present state of our knowledge.

(4.) Our fourth hypothesis is true in a modified sense. A considerable number of the words common to the LXX. and New Testament *are* derived words, formed by the writers of the LXX. To the extent covered by these words, there is an influence of the one vocabulary on the other. But the whole number is exceedingly small in relation to the entire vocabulary of the New Testament. Moreover, we may well believe that these words would have become part of the vocabulary of the New Testament writers, although they had never read a page of the LXX. The words were absolutely necessary for Jews. That is to say, there were certain important Hebrew conceptions connected with national customs or worship or tradition which had to be expressed in Greek. Some of these may have been translated into the foreign language before there was a trace of the LXX. But the great majority of them was, no doubt, due to this version. Immediately, however, they would pass into the current Greek used by Jews, and by this means often into the general vocabulary of the Eastern peoples.

(5.) The fifth supposition is also true, in the case before us, in a modified sense. We have already seen that the creation of theological terms by the New Testament writers certainly followed the analogy of the Greek words used by the translators of the LXX. to set forth the conceptions of Hebrew theology. In this sphere there can be no question in regard to the influence of the LXX. on the New Testament. In some cases, as our instances have shown, there appears to be a deliberate stereotyping of usage which henceforward becomes part and parcel of the Jewish-Greek vocabulary. Yet even here it is more generally the basis which remains. The superstructure reared by the Christian writers shows marked divergences. The main modification to be noted in this connection is the same as that which was found necessary in our last hypothesis. Outside the strict sphere of theological terminology there is a fairly large group of words, as has been shown, common to the LXX. and New Testament, with other authors, which, at first sight, appear to have significations entirely peculiar to these two groups of writings. These words designate a variety of ideas, some referring to matters of physical or everyday life, others denoting moral qualities and the like. But the more carefully these special senses are examined, the more uniformly will it be found either that they are peculiar colloquial significations which may have existed for long in the popular language, or that they themselves, and words with senses cognate to them, occur here and there in isolated contemporary writers; or else that in many cases the special meanings are so closely connected with the ordinary sense, as to depend chiefly on the context in which the word may be found.

(6.) It is difficult to say whether this last possibility can be regarded as actually verified in connection with our inquiry or not. It is hard to decide whether there are local peculiarities to be found in the New Testament vocabulary. Certainly traces do exist of words which the oldest tradition connects with Alexandria. And we know it was a centre of the mixed language of later times. We can safely regard some of the unique features of the language of the LXX. as " Alexandrian." In the New Testament, such influences are harder to trace. If there are " Alexandrian " words in the New Testament, they are so sporadic in their appearance that we should attribute them to the general current of the Greek language as it manifests itself in New Testament times, rather than to the direct influence of the LXX. Perhaps we may look for such peculiarities with greater probability among the *forms* than among the words which compose the New Testament vocabulary.

CHAPTER XI

COLLOQUIAL GREEK, THE LANGUAGE OF THE LXX. AND OF THE NEW TESTAMENT

No one who reads the LXX. and New Testament with open eyes can fail to be at once struck with the fact that there is some general characteristic about their language which marks it off distinctly from that of the rest of Greek books. And it is just this common and striking element which is apt to give the impression that the New Testament owes its particular type of speech directly to the LXX. Perhaps it may be said that if the LXX. had never been written, the New Testament writings would have shown a greater harshness of style and clumsiness of expression than is actually found there. But as regards the respective vocabularies, they are both children of the same parent, namely, the colloquial Greek of the time. This is the secret of their striking resemblance.

Unfortunately our knowledge of the colloquial language from other sources is fragmentary in the extreme. But the evidence which *is* extant goes solidly to prove the essentially vernacular character of Biblical Greek. How much lies concealed from us is well exemplified by stray Greek words which occur in Latin authors, as, *e.g.*, in

COLLOQUIAL GREEK, THE LANGUAGE OF LXX. AND N.T. 147

Cicero's *Letters*,[1] where a considerable list of words is found, including terms like ἀθέτησις, ἐμπερπερεύομαι, σκυλμός, συζήτησις, and others, whose use by Cicero proves their common occurrence in the language of everyday life, though they are found in no Greek book. So also, from time to time, the Inscriptions show us words of which the very meaning is proof that their use was not exceptional.

We have already given brief discussions of elements in the vocabularies both of the LXX. and New Testament which bear on their "Colloquialism." This was illustrated notably by lists of vernacular words common to both; their fondness for diminutives; their frequent use of words, originally strong, in a weakened sense; and, above all, their remarkable points of contact both with the vocabulary of Aristophanes and the Fragments of the Comic poets. We may recall the statistics—

Of words found in Aristophanes and exceedingly seldom in any other Greek author—

55 occur in the vocabulary of the New Testament;

and *31 of these* in the vocabulary of the LXX.

Of words found in the Fragments of the Comic poets, and almost nowhere else in Greek literature—

151 occur in the vocabulary of the New Testament;

and about *98 of these* in the vocabulary of the LXX.

Of course, in the case of Aristophanes, some of these words may occur where he is intentionally imitating the vernacular, but it need hardly be said that this only makes them more valuable for our comparison. In con-

[1] Cf. T. K. Abbott, *Essays on the Original Texts of the Old and New Testaments*, 1891, p. 87.

nection with these lists it must also be noted that if an exhaustive examination were made of the vocabulary of the LXX. it would certainly reveal a far greater resemblance than our own scrutiny has been able to bring out, seeing that our comparisons have only taken in words found in the New Testament.

It is not hard to see how this special "colloquial" colouring is so prominent in the Biblical language. Plainly, from the earliest days there existed in Greek-speaking regions a mode of speech separated both from the literary language and that used by cultivated men, which belonged to the common people. Grammarians observe that the existence of syncopated forms in Homer, such as δῶ for δῶμα, ἄλφι for ἄλφιτον, similar phenomena in Hesiod, such as βρῖ for βριαρόν, and the like, and various other appearances in writers like Alcman and Epicharmus, point to an ancient popular language, not confined to any particular locality. Many forms and expressions in Aristophanes, which he puts into the mouths of particular characters, go to confirm the idea. This special vernacular type of speech would, of course, exist all through the history of the Greek literature and language. And certainly its prevalence and growth must have been enormously aided by Alexander's conquests. All the forces dominant at that particular period in the Greek of the Macedonian conquerors tended to give permanence, and even prestige, to the speech of the people. Seeing that now, even the literary language of books had become unregulated and lax, the barrier between the refined spoken language and that of the mass of the people, which must at all times be fluctuating, would tend more and more to disappear.

How, then, would this condition of things bear upon a foreign nation, introduced, as it were, to a new tongue? Our own observation may serve to guide us in this matter. Everyone knows that a German, for example, who may have to live in an English-speaking country for professional or business purposes, even should he be a man of superior education, delights above all else to acquire a certain mastery of the more colloquial part of the English language. And in conversation, almost contrary to what one might expect, he goes out of his way to use the most "popular," not to say "vulgar" expressions. Is it going too far to attribute this trait of human nature to the Jews who first came into contact with Greek?

But this is only one element in the process. Jews then, as now, were eager traders, if they were anything. And the language of commercial intercourse must ·be, from the nature of the case, a plain, unrefined, hackneyed mode of speech, ready to open its doors to words which are often mere "slang" expressions, a strictly commonplace language, intelligible in all business circles. Unquestionably this was the type of Greek which first met the Jews in Alexandria and in all the trading centres of the East. But from the first they were extraordinarily conservative as regards education, and the wealthier among them especially so. In this way, those of them who might be expected to reach a higher culture in literature, and thus come into contact with Greek in its refined and pure form, would be, in most cases, the very class whom the traditions of their fathers and their pride of national feeling would exclude from all such influences. Therefore it is not astonishing that the books of the LXX. display so marked a resemblance to the language of the street. This is made all the more peculiar to a reader by its blending with the cumbrous terms of Hebrew ritual and theology.

As time went on, the colloquial language would necessarily be modified in various directions. As has been already noted, it must have come to be the language of educated people. For anything like a return to the refined Attic dialect of the Golden Age of Athens could at this period be regarded only as an affectation, too artificial to escape detection. Yet these facts did, as we know, exert an important influence on the colloquial language itself. Its employment by men of education reacted upon it. We do not mean to say that Greek as spoken by the populace became purer, but there came into existence a special type of the vernacular, that used by cultivated people. This was distinguished by forms less grotesque than those of the more "vulgar" type. Shades and refinements of distinction were more carefully attended to. Semi-literary words belonging to the "Common" dialect, and put into circulation by the authors who employed it, are found more frequently.

Now, it need hardly be said that men of Jewish birth were affected by this development. And there were special reasons that it should be so. As they gradually became naturalised in the countries of their adoption, and were unconsciously influenced by their surroundings, many of their prejudices completely vanished. They began to participate with enthusiasm in the higher education of their time. Soon great numbers of them became thoroughly Hellenised. Not only so. Long residence in Greek-speaking countries gave them a thorough mastery of the language. Each successive generation, born amidst Greek influences, acquired more power, more intelligence, and more taste in speaking Greek. Greek became a common language in Palestine itself; and the more gifted and acute the particular Jew might be, the more likely was it that he should strive to speak the popular colloquial language in a refined manner.

A most interesting example of the process we have been discussing is shown by a comparison of the language of the LXX., in general, with that of the New Testament. The results of such a comparison could not be better expressed than in the words of Mr. Geldart: "The Greek of the New Testament, however popular, familiar, and simple, is by no means so vulgar, so nearly a vernacular, as that of the LXX. We miss, with few exceptions, and those chiefly to be found in the Apocalypse, forms like εἶδα, etc., which must have existed in the New Testament age, because they are preserved in modern Greek to the present. It was familiar and popular, but not vernacular; it adopted the homely expressions, but did not, as a whole, let itself down to the grammatical level of the common people, like a modern Greek newspaper, which is familiar enough to be readily intelligible, but not enough so to be vulgar; neither altogether the spoken language of the common people, nor yet by a long way the book language of the learned."[1]

[1] *Modern Greek Language in its Relation to Ancient Greek*, App. I. p. 180.

CHAPTER XII

CORROBORATION OF THE COLLOQUIAL CHARACTER OF THE LANGUAGE OF THE LXX. AND NEW TESTAMENT BY THE PHENOMENA OF MODERN GREEK

THE position we have sought to maintain in the preceding section as regards the "Colloquialism" of the vocabularies both of the LXX. and the New Testament receives striking corroboration in a very important direction. Modern Greek, as spoken to-day, is, of course, in its main elements nothing else than the descendant of the old vernacular speech. And so it is in organic connection with the popular language as it prevailed in the days when the LXX. and the New Testament were written. No doubt it has undergone numerous modifications both in grammar and vocabulary, yet in its essential character it is the same language as that which the Jews learned amidst the bustling life of Alexandria. In spite of the many centuries which separate them, there is nothing like the same difference between the Greek of to-day and that spoken of in the times of the LXX. and New Testament, as between the latter and the language of Demosthenes. Accordingly, we might expect that more or less light would be thrown on the relation of the vocabularies of the LXX. and New

Testament to the colloquial language by the phenomena of modern Greek. Nor are we disappointed. The following short lists, compiled almost at random, are a sample of the important evidence which the modern language brings to bear on our subject.

Nouns

ἀνθρακιά Accent shows it to be a vernacular form. Occurs in N.T. Found in mod. Gk.

ἀρχηγός. In mod. Gk. = leader, in the ordinary sense. Similar use in LXX. and N.T. Rarely in Class. Lit.

βασίλισσα. LXX. and N.T. Inscr. of Sigeum, B.C. 270. Late form for βασίλεια. Mod. Gk.

βροχή. Late word. N.T. and LXX. Mod. Gk = rain.

γεῦμα. In mod. Gk. = dinner; cf. γεύομαι in N.T. = eat, take food. γεῦμα in Class. Lit. = taste.

δῶμα. In mod. Gk. = terrace. Cf. its use in LXX. and N.T. = flat roof of house.

ἐρεθισμός. In mod. Gk. = excitement, in a good sense. Cf. verb ἐρεθίζω, used in a good sense in the N.T., while in a bad from Homer down. In ordinary Greek, ἐρεθισμός is usually a medical term in Hippocrates.

ἡγούμενος. Mod. Gk. = superior of a monastery. In LXX. and N.T. = leader.

θέλησις. Mod. Gk. = will. So LXX. and N.T. Pollux calls it a "vulgarism."

θυσιαστήριον Mod. Gk. = altar. So LXX. and N.T.

(τὰ) ἱμάτια = the clothes. (Very seldom in Class. Lit.) Common in mod. Gk., the LXX., and N.T.

καιρός. Mod. Gk. = weather. Cf. its constant use in the LXX. and N.T. = season, in our sense, especially in phrases like καιροὶ καρποφόροι, etc. Our word "season" has a similar connotation of weather.

καθηγητής. Mod. Gk. = professor. In N.T. = master, teacher. Once in this sense in Dion. Hal., and apparently also in Plutarch.

κατάλυμα. Mod. Gk. = lodging. So in LXX. and N.T., where it has also the sense of "guest-chamber." Something like this meaning in Polybius and Diodorus.

καύσων. Mod. Gk. = heat. In this sense repeatedly in LXX. and N.T. Apparently also once in Lucian. Dioscor. 1. 21. 149, has it as a medical term = heat in the stomach.

κιβώτιον. Mod. Gk. = box. Cf. κιβωτός in LXX. and N.T. = the ark. Both words in Aristophanes.

κοράσιον. Mod. Gk. = girl. So LXX., and N.T.: "cum nulla εὐτελισμοῦ significatione." This use also in Arrian.

κρεββατί. Mod. Gk. = bed. So precisely κράββατος in N.T. Also found in the Comic poets Crito and Rhinthon. Lat. "*grabatus*," in Martial.

μονή. Mod. Gk. = monastery. In N.T. = dwelling-place. Pausanias uses it = station.

ξενοδοχεῖον. Mod. Gk. = hotel. Cf. verb ξενοδοχέω in LXX. and N.T. = entertain hospitably. Verb also in Dion. Cass.

ὀπτασία. Mod. Gk. = vision. So in N.T. and LXX. Appar. also in Anthology.

παιδίον. Mod. Gk. = boy. So in LXX. and N.T. Scarcely in this colourless sense in Class. Lit.

πρόσκομμα. Mod. Gk. = obstacle, hindrance. So N.T. and LXX.

προσφάγιον. Mod. Gk. = that which is eaten with bread. So = French "*fricot*." N.T. = fish (as being eaten with bread). Cf. Inscr. of Iulis, 130 B.C.: προσφαγίωι χρέσθαι (κ)ατὰ (τ)ὰ (π)άτρια.

ῥῆγμα = πτῶσις (of a house). So in N.T. Cf. mod. Gk. ῥήχνω = ῥίπτω.

τελωνεῖον. Mod. Gk. = custom-house. So precisely in N.T.: τελώνιον. Also in the Comic poet Posidippus.

ὑπουργός. Mod. Gk. = minister (of government). In LXX. = *adjutor, qui operam navat; minister, administer* (Schleusner). Used there of one who, while a servant, is a free man.

φωλεά. Mod. Gk. = nest. Cf. φωλεός in N.T. = burrow, lurking-hole of animals.

CORROBORATION OF LXX. AND N.T. BY MODERN GREEK 155

Verbs, etc. etc.

ἀποκρίνομαι In the passive in mod. Gk. = answer. So LXX. and N.T.

βαστάζω. Mod. Gk. = φέρω (in colourless sense). So often in N.T.

βρέχει. Mod. Gk. = ὕει. So repeatedly in LXX. and N.T.

γεμίζω. Mod. Gk. = fill (non-technical sense). So LXX. and N.T.

γευματίζω. Mod. Gk. = dine. Cf. γεύομαι in N.T. = eat.

ἐγγίζω. Mod. Gk. = approach. This sense frequent in LXX. and N.T. Also in Polybius.

ἐνώπιον. Mod. Gk. = in the presence of. So LXX. and N.T.

ἐπισκέπτομαι. Mod. Gk. = visit. Same sense in LXX. and N.T. A few times in Class. Lit. (and almost always = visit the sick).

ἐπιστρέφω. Mod. Gk. = return. So in LXX. and N.T. Hippoc. uses it of the *recurrence* of an illness.

εὐφραίνομαι. Mod. Gk. uses it of *festive* enjoyment. So in LXX. and N.T.

θεωρέω. Mod. Gk. θωρῶ = see (simply). θεωρέω used in precisely same sense in LXX. and N.T.

κοιμῶμαι. Mod. Gk. = sleep. Constantly in LXX. (especially) and N.T. = εὕδω, καθεύδω.

κομβόω. Mod. Gk. = button. Cf. ἐγκομβόομαι = fasten on one's self, in N.T. The latter also in Epicharmus and Apollodorus Carystius (*Com.*).

ὁμιλέω. Mod. Gk. = converse with. So in LXX. and N.T. Also in Josephus and Xenophon.

παιδεύω. Mod. Gk. = chastise. So frequently in LXX. and N.T.

πιάζω. Mod. Gk. πιάνω = seize, apprehend. πιάζω has the same sense in LXX. and N.T.

συζητέω. Mod. Gk. = discuss, dispute. So regularly in N.T.

τρώγω. Mod. Gk. = eat (simply). Same use in N.T.

ὑπάγω. Mod. Gk. = εἶμι. So constantly in N.T. Similar use in the Comic poets.

φθάνω. Mod. Gk. = arrive, come. Very common in this exact meaning in the LXX. and N.T. Also found with the same sense in Philo and Plutarch.

χορτάζω, χορτάζομαι. Mod. Gk. = feed. Constantly in this sense in LXX. and N.T. Same meaning often found in the Comic writers.

ψηλαφάω. Mod. Gk. = ψαύειν. Same sense frequent in LXX. and N.T. Apparently in Xenophon = pat, or stroke (horses).

CHAPTER XIII

EXAMINATION OF PECULIAR FORMS WHICH GO TO PROVE THE "COLLOQUIAL" CHARACTER OF THE LANGUAGE OF THE LXX. AND NEW TESTAMENT

THERE remains, still, a class of facts to be glanced at which is of the first importance in shedding light on the essentially "colloquial" character of the LXX. and New Testament. We refer to a large group of peculiar *forms* which make their appearance in these writings, in inscriptions, in late writers, and often in modern Greek.

The range of literature within which they are found makes it plain that they are of a "popular" character. There are considerable differences as to the writings which contain them. Many which are present in inscriptions, the LXX., and Christian apocryphal literature are not met with in the New Testament. This is exactly what we should have expected from the general superiority of New Testament diction. Still, sufficient instances occur to show how thoroughly the New Testament is a "popular" book.

Distinctions must be made between the various types which, for convenience' sake, are included in the same group. Some are mere variations from the ordinary spelling. At first sight it might seem as if objections could be raised against placing reliance on the orthography of our earliest MSS., so far as regards the New Testament. But, as Dr. Hort well shows (*N.T.* ii. 355), the probabilities are unfavourable to the hypothesis of the introduction of such forms by the transcribers of the New Testament: "In the fourth and following centuries, and even during a great part of the third, a natural result of the social position of Christians would be a tendency of scribes to root out supposed vulgarisms, as is known to have been the case in the revisions of the Old Latin as regards grammatical forms as well as vocabulary."

The rest of the forms under consideration are, for the most part, anomalous tense-endings and, in a few cases, special modifications in verb- and noun-formations.

(1.) στήκω. Constantly in N.T. and LXX. = ἵστημι. Cf. στέκω, in mod. Gk. in same sense. A form ἰστέκω is also cited by Ducange. So in the mod. language, θέτω = τίθημι, δίδω = δίδωμι.

Apparently, it is almost a rule in modern Greek that while verbs in -μι are used in the more refined literary style, in ordinary conversation the same verbs appear in -ω. στήκω is common in the writers of the Middle Ages. Also a form στήνω.

There are, besides, forms in the N.T. such as ἀφίομεν (Luke), ἤφιεν (Mark), ἀφίονται (John), συνίουσιν (Matt.), συνίων (Rom.), which presuppose the colloquial verbs ἀφίω and συνίω.

(2.) πίεσαι, φάγεσαι. These 2nd pers. sing. forms of irregular futures in -ομαι occur together in Luke 17. 8 : μετὰ ταῦτα φάγεσαι καὶ πίεσαι σύ.

The same and similar forms repeatedly in the LXX., *e.g.* Ruth 2. 14: φάγεσαι τῶν ἄρτων; Ezek. 4. 11: ὕδωρ ἐν μέτρῳ πίεσαι. But, besides, the 2nd pers. sing. *of the present indicative pass.* (or *mid.*) is found in the same formation both in N.T. and LXX., *e.g.* Rom. 11. 18: κατακαυχᾶσαι, etc.; 1 Kings 14. 6: ἀποξενοῦσαι.

In the "common" Greek of to-day, precisely the same endings are found in the 2nd pers. sing. present indic. pass., in ordinary verbs as -εσαι, in contracted verbs -εῖσαι, -ᾶσαι; *e.g.* φαίνεσαι, πατεῖσαι, καυχᾶσαι.

These forms are evidently the originals of the usual contracted 2nd pers. sing., and must have been handed down unchanged in the popular language from a remote antiquity.

(3.) Abnormal imperfect terminations in verbs ending in -μι. Thus from δίδωμι: διεδίδετο (N.T. Acts), παρεδίδετο (N.T. 1 Cor.), ἐδίδετο (LXX. Ex. 5. 13). Perhaps the same tendency is seen in the frequently-found "vulgar" form διδοῦσιν for διδόασιν, on which Lobeck says: "transmigravit hæc forma ex Iade in vulgarem, quam dicere solemus, linguam omnium dialectorum commune diversorium."

(4.) ἤμην. Repeatedly in N.T. as impf. of εἰμί, *e.g.* Matt. 25. 35: ξένος ἤμην καὶ συνηγάγετέ με. It is striking to find this the regular form of the impf. of mod. Gk. εἶμαι = εἰμί.

(5.) A very important group of forms in connection with the present inquiry is that consisting of "strong" Aorists with "weak" terminations. A few of these have a sort of recognition in Class. Lit., as εἶπα, ἤνεγκα, and ἔπεσα, but the usage receives enormous extension in the LXX. and N.T., *e.g.* 2 Kings 10. 14: εἶδαν; Esth. 5. 4: ἐλθάτω; 2 Kings 17. 20: εὗραν, etc. etc.; Acts 16. 40: ἐξῆλθαν.

εἶδαν, ἀνεῖλαν, ἔλθατε, ἀνεῦραν, εὕραμεν, etc. etc., are all well attested. This termination is also found with the imperf. in the LXX. and N.T., *e.g.* Mark 8. 7: εἶχαν.

This is one of the most marked of the "colloquial" forms which crept into the late literature of Greece. Isolated instances occur in Philo, Plutarch, Pausanias and Lucian. Menander has εὑράμην. The usage spread and became common in the Roman and Byzantine periods. Thus from the Roman period we find in Inscriptions instances like ἔσχα (*C.I.A.* iii. 1363. 5), εὑράμην (900. 6), ἤλπιζα (Kaibel, *Epigram. Græc.* 167. 5). Byzantine writers like Malalas have ἐκβάλαι (= ἐκβαλεῖν), ἀνεῖλαν, etc.

By 300 A.D. this formation has become frequent in the imperf., as the Inscrr. show, *e.g.* ἤφερα (for ἔφερον) and the like.

In the colloquial Greek of to-day both the imperf. (of the uncontracted verb) and strong Aorist end in -*a*, *e.g.* φεύγω, impf. ἔφευγα, Aor. ἔφυγα. The first and third persons plural have also the -*a* vowel.

(6.) Common to the LXX. and N.T. is the curious termination -οσαν in Aorists and imperfects, *e.g.* in N.T. εἴχοσαν, John 15. 22; παρελάβοσαν, 2 Thess. 3. 6; ἐδολιοῦσαν, Rom. 3. 13. In LXX. ἐκρίνοσαν, Ex. 18. 26; ἐφάγοσαν, Josh. 5. 11, etc. etc.

The old Grammarians give various origins for this form, some designating it Chalcidian, others Boeotian, others again Aeolic. It is found in the Comic poet

CHARACTER OF LANGUAGE OF LXX. AND N.T. 161

Posidippus, who has εἴχοσαν. Also in Scymnus Chius (quoted by Mullach), ἔσχοσαν. The history of the form is traceable in a fragmentary way. ἀπήλθοσαν occurs in an Inscr. of Thisbæ, 170 B.C. (Dittenb. *Syll*. 226. 40), παρελάβοσαν in one of Delos, 180 B.C. (Dittenb. *Syll*. 367. 112). In the Byzantine writers it is of frequent occurrence, *e.g.* εἴδοσαν, Niceph. *Greg*. 6. 5. 113; παρήλθοσαν, Nicet. *Chon*. 153, etc. etc. The form survives in mod. Gk. in the 3 plur. impf. of contracted verbs, *e.g.* ἐπατοῦσαν from πατέω, ἐδολιοῦσαν from δολιόω. These very forms occur in the LXX., *e.g.* Ex. 33. 8: κατενοοῦσαν = κατενόουν; Gen. 6. 4: ἐγέννωσαν = ἐγέννων. With these terminations in -οσαν may be compared the Aor. and impf. forms, ἀφίλεσαν, ἐλαμβάνεσαν, in Greek Papyri in the British Museum.

(7.) -αν for -ασι in the 3 plur. of perfects.

Sextus Empir. (*adv. Gramm.* 213) says: λέξις ἡ παρ' Ἀλεξανδρεῦσιν ἐλήλυθαν καὶ ἀπελήλυθαν.

But there is abundant evidence that this was a "popular" form of much wider range. It is frequent in the LXX., *e.g.* Deut. 11. 7: ἑώρακαν; Isa. 5. 29: παρέστηκαν, etc. So also in the N.T.: ἔγνωκαν (John), εἰσελήλυθαν (James), ἀπέσταλκαν (Acts), ἑώρακαν (Col.), etc. etc.

Lycophron has πέφρικαν; ἔοργαν occurs in the Batryomachia, and πέφυκαν in Democritus.

The Inscriptions afford important evidence of the wide area over which the usage extends. Thus in an Inscr. of Smyrna, 235 B.C. (Dittenb. *Syll*. 171), we have παρείληφαν. In one of Lakonia, *c.* 70 B.C., there occur διατετέλεκαν, εἴσχηκαν, and πεποίηκαν (Dittenb. *Syll.* 255).

(8.) Another form, which is almost certainly " popular," occurs in the present and Aorists optative.

The original ending -σαν appears in the 3 plur. active of these tenses. Phavorinus holds the form to be Aeolic, but extant evidence does not seem to support the hypothesis. It appears rather to be related to the group examined in (6).

Instances do not occur in the N.T., but they are common in the LXX., *e.g.* Deut. 1. 44: ποιήσαισαν; Ps. 103. 35: ἐκλείποισαν; Job 18. 9: ἔλθοισαν. In an Inscription of Delphi, παρέχοισαν is found.

(9.) What may be apparently regarded as a form of "vulgar" speech is the appearance of a pseudo-future subjunct. in the LXX. and N.T., *e.g.* a fut. indic. used for the Aor. subjunct., and written with the vowels of the subjunct. Cf. Luke 7. 4: ἀξιός ἐστιν ᾧ παρέξῃ τοῦτο; 1 Cor. 13. 3: ἵνα . . . καυθήσωμαι; cf. in LXX. Gen. 2. 17: φάγησθε. But in all these cases the readings are so varying, that it is unsafe to build any conclusion on them.

(10.) An isolated instance of a "popular" form is κάθου, as imperat. of κάθημαι. It is found in the LXX. as, *e.g.*, Ps. 110. 1: κάθου ἐκ δεξιῶν μου. Also in the N.T., *e.g.* Acts 2. 34; Mark 12. 36. This form, contracted from κάθεσο, is the present imperative of κάθημαι in modern Greek. It is also found in the Fragments of the Comic writers.

(11.) It is hardly necessary to do more than note two characteristics of the "popular" spelling which occur constantly in the N.T. and LXX. The one is the interchange of ι and ει, ει being used to designate the long sound of ι, e.g. σειροῖς, 2 Pet. 2. 4, etc.; cf. the forms γείνομαι and γεινώσκω, which have excellent attestation. So in Inscrr., e.g. ἐμεσείτευσαν, C.I.A. 488. 17 (30 B.C.).

On the other hand, there is the tendency to shorten long sounds, so that ι is found for ει. Thus λιτουργεῖν is the best attested reading in the N.T. So also πιθοῖς in 1 Cor. 2. 4, and other instances *passim*. A similar result is given by the Inscrr., which show that in Roman times λιτουργεῖν was the common spelling; cf. also πιθαρχοῦντες, C.I.A. 471. 17 (100 B.C.).

But this tendency is best exhibited by the large class of substantives which shorten -εία to -ία, as ἀρεσκία, ἑρμηνία, μεθοδία κ.τ.λ.

(12.) An interesting instance of a "vulgar" form is that in which a "ν" is added to the accus. sing. of nouns of the third declension. There is no *certain* instance in the N.T., but it is very common in the LXX., e.g. Ex. 10. 4: ἀκρίδαν; Ruth 4. 12: γυναῖκαν; 1 Kings 22. 11: ἱερέαν.

The Inscrr. also exhibit this peculiarity, e.g. Thessalian Inscr. of second cent.: τὸν ἄνδραν.

It occurs, too, in those of the later empire, e.g. πατρίδαν (C.I.A. iii. 1379. 10), χάριταν (Kaibel, *Epigram. Græc.* 167. 6). The form survives in the "common" language of to-day.

(13.) It only remains to point out some "popular" spellings in the Biblical writers.

a. Harsh concurrences permitted *e.a.* λήμψομαι (Winer compares Ionic λάμψομαι), σφακνυγεῖν, εὐχωρῶν.

b. Addition of superfluous letters, *e.g.* ἐκχθές, ἐκχυννόμενον, ἔσσπειρε.

c. Omission of letters, *e.g.* δυσεβής, ἐρύσατο κ.τ.λ.

These or similar forms occur with the best attestation in the LXX. and N.T., and are also exhibited by many Inscrr.

It is needless to give, in closing, an elaborate summary of the results to which our investigation has led us, as this has been already done. But the main conclusions can be put in a few sentences.

The LXX. is the first entire group of writings composed in the colloquial language of everyday life. Seeing that it is a literal translation of Hebrew books, and that it has been carried out by men of Jewish birth, it is deeply impregnated with Semitic characteristics. Yet these do not prevent it from exhibiting clearly the condition and tendencies of the popular Greek of its time. On the one hand, it has many elements in common with the writers of the κοινὴ διάλεκτος; on the other, it is often a transcript of the vernacular. But the predominant features in its vocabulary are—

(*a*) The creation of a theological terminology rendered necessary by the original of which it is a translation; and

(*b*) The expression in Greek form of special Jewish conceptions and customs due to the same cause.

There can be no question that its vocabulary has influenced that of the New Testament. The earliest Christian writers, in proclaiming the new faith, had to express in words deep theological ideas, unheard of in the old world. It was natural that, in making this attempt, they should take for their model a vocabulary already formed. These writers, moreover, were Jews. Their whole view of things was penetrated with Hebrew modes of thought. Accordingly, they could not fail to make copious use of a type of language already adapted to their special requirements.

But the influence of the LXX. on the vocabulary of the New Testament must not be exaggerated. Caution is necessary in determining that which is to be regarded as *usage* in Biblical Greek, seeing that the LXX. is a translation done by unskilful hands, and that ignorance of Greek or ignorance of Hebrew is often responsible for phenomena of vocabulary which are peculiar to the Biblical language. When we consider the exceptional importance of the Greek Bible to the New Testament writers, the astonishing fact is that its influence on their vocabulary is not incomparably greater than it is found to be.

That which really sets the LXX. and New Testament, as Greek books, in a class by themselves, is the colloquial language in which both are written. Though the vocabulary of the New Testament moves on a higher plane, it is essentially "popular" in character, and both groups of writings acquire, from the linguistic point of view, a unique importance, as the only literary monuments extant of the vernacular Greek of the post-Alexandrine period.

But, besides, this popular spoken language, as exhibited by the LXX. and New Testament, is of exceptional value for another reason, inasmuch as it connects the "oral tradition" of the past with the ordinary vernacular of to-day, and reveals with startling clearness that wonderful organic unity which makes the language of Greece, through all its complex developments, a living, undivided whole.

LIST OF AUTHORITIES

CHIEFLY REFERRED TO OR CONSULTED

ABBOTT, T. K., Essays on the Original Texts of the Old and New Testaments. Longmans, 1891.

BERNHARDY, Grundriss der Griechischen Litteratur. Band I.

BLEEK, Der Hebräer-Brief. Berlin, 1828–1840.

BRUDER, Concordance to the New Testament. 2 vols. Leipzig: Bredt, 1880.

CARR, Notes on St. Luke. "St. Matthew" in "Cambridge Greek Testament for Colleges."

CLASSICAL REVIEW, vols. i.–iv. Various Articles.

CORPUS INSCRIPTIONUM ATTICARUM. Ed. by Kirchhoff, Koehler, Dittenberger. Berlin.

CREMER, Biblico-Theological Lexicon of New Testament Greek. English edition, T. & T. Clark, 1886.

DITTENBERGER, W., Sylloge Inscriptionum Græcarum. Leipzig, 1883.

DUNBAR, Concordance to the Comedies and Fragments of Aristophanes. Oxford, 1882.

EWALD, History of Israel, vol. v.

EXPOSITOR, 1875–1891. Various Articles.

FIELD, F., The Hexapla of Origen. 2 vols. Oxford, 1875.

GEBHARDT, O., The New Testament in Greek. Tischendorf's Recension, ed. by Von Gebhardt. Leipzig: Tauchnitz, 1886.

GELDART, E. M., The Modern Greek Language in its Relation to Ancient Greek. Oxford, 1870.

GESENIUS, Hebrew and Chaldee Lexicon.
GREEN, T. S., Grammar of the New Testament. Bagster, 1862.
GREGORY, C. R., Prolegomena to the New Testament in Greek, by C. Tischendorf. 8th edition. Leipzig: Hinrichs, 1884–1894.
GRAETZ, Geschichte der Juden. Band III.
GRIMM, W., Greek-English Lexicon of the New Testament. English edition, by J. Thayer. T. & T. Clark, 1888.
GRIMM, C. L. Das Buch der Weisheit. Erklaert von C. L. Grimm. Leipzig: Hirzel, 1860. Das 2, 3, 4, Buch der Maccabäer. 1857.
GUILLEMARD, W. H., Hebraisms in the Greek New Testament. 1879.
HATCH, E., Essays in Biblical Greek. Oxford, 1889.
HATCH and REDPATH, Concordance to the Septuagint, Parts I., II. Oxford, 1892–1893.
HODY, De Bibliorum Textibus Originalibus. Oxford, 1705.
HOLDEN, Editions of Plutarch's "Lives." Camb. Univ. Press.
HOLTZMANN, H. J., Die Synoptiker. Leipzig: Engelmann, 1863.
KOCK, T., Comicorum Atticorum Fragmenta. 3 vols. Leipzig: Teubner, 1880–1888.
LOBECK, C. A., Phrynichi Eclogæ. Leipzig, 1820.
MEISTERHANS, K., Grammatik der Attischen Inschriften. Berlin: Weidmann, 1888.
MEINEKE, Fragmenta Comicorum Græcorum. Berlin, 1841.
MULLACH, F. W. A., Grammatik der Griechischen Vulgarsprache. Berlin: Dümmler, 1856.
PATON, Inscriptions of Cos. Oxford, 1891.
PSICHARI, J., Études Néo-grecques. Paris, 1892.
RUTHERFORD, W. G., The New Phrynichus. Macmillan, 1881.
SALMON, G., Introduction to the New Testament. Murray, 1889.
SCHLEUSNER, J. F., Lexicon to the Septuagint. London, 1829.
SCHWEIGHÄUSER, Lexicon Polybianum.
SIEGFRIED, C., Untersuchungen über die Gräcität Philo's Jena: Dufft, 1875.

AUTHORITIES CHIEFLY REFERRED TO OR CONSULTED 169

SIMCOX, W. H., The Language of the New Testament. 1889. The Writers of the New Testament. 1890. Hodder & Stoughton.

SOPHOCLES, E. A., Greek Lexicon of the Roman and Byzantine Periods. Boston, 1870.

STURZ, F. G., De Dialecto Macedonica et Alexandrina Libri. 1808.

SWETE, H. B., The Old Testament in Greek according to the Septuagint. 3 vols. Camb. 1887–1894.

THIERSCH, H. G., De Pentateuchi Versione Alexandrina. Erlangen, 1841.

TISCHENDORF, Vetus Testamentum Græce.

TROMMIUS, A., Concordance to the Septuagint. 2 vols. 1718.

VINCENT and DICKSON, Handbook to Modern Greek (with Appendix by Jebb). Macmillan, 1887.

WEISS, Introduction to the New Testament. Eng. trans. Hodder & Stoughton, 1887–1888.

WESTCOTT, B. F., Introduction to the Gospels. The New Testament in Greek. 2 vols. (Westcott and Hort.)

WELLHAUSEN, art. "Septuagint" in Encyclopædia Britannica.

WINER, Grammar of New Testament Greek. Trans. by Moulton. T. & T. Clark, 1882.

WYTTENBACH, Index Verborum in Plutarcho.

ZEZSCHWITZ, Profangräcität und Biblischer Sprachgeist. Leipzig: Hinrichs, 1859.

INDEX OF GREEK WORDS DISCUSSED

ἀδελφός, 95.
ἀδυνατέω, 124.
ἀκροβυστία, 111.
ἀλίσγημα, 129.
ἀμφιάζω, 129.
ἀναθεματίζω, 117.
ἀναφέρω, 103.
ἀνθρακιά, 153.
ἀνθρωπάρεσκος, 115.
ἀντίληψις, 96.
ἀποδεκατόω, 117.
ἀποκαλύπτω, 104.
ἀποκεφαλίζω, 130.
ἀποκρίνομαι, 155.
ἀποκρίνω, 124.
ἀποστάσιον, 121.
ἀρχηγός, 153.

βάλλω, 81.
βασίλισσα, 153.
βαστάζω, 155.
βεβηλόω, 117.
βουνός, 44.
βρέχω, 39, 155.
βροχή, 153.

γεμίζω, 155.
γεῦμα, 153.
γευματίζω, 155.
γλωσσόκομον, 39.
γογγύζω, 39.

διάβολος, 97.

δικιαιόω, 104.
δόξα, 97.
δῶμα, 121, 153.

ἐγγίζω, 155.
ἐγκαινίζω, 118.
ἔθνος, 98.
εἰρήνη, 98.
ἐκκλησία, 99.
ἔκστασις, 121.
ἐμπαιγμός, 130.
ἐνώπιον, 155.
ἐνωτίζομαι, 130.
ἐξολεθρεύω, 130.
ἐξομολογέω, 118.
ἐξυπνίζω, 131.
ἐπιγαμβρεύω, 118.
ἐπισκέπτομαι, 105, 155.
ἐπισκοπή, 112.
ἐπιστρέφω, 155.
ἐρεθισμός, 153.
εὐδοκία, 131.
εὐλογέω, 105.
εὐφραίνομαι, 155.
ἐφημερία, 112.

ἡγούμενος, 153.
ἤμην, 159.

θέλησις, 153.
θεωρέω, 155.
θροέω, 126.
θυσιαστήριον, 153.

ἱερατεύειν, 119.
ἱεράτευμα, 131.
ἱλαστήριον, 113.
ἱμάτια, 153.

καθηγητής, 153.
κάθου, 162.
καιρός, 153.
κακία, 100.
κατάλυμα, 154.
καταπέτασμα, 113.
καταστολή, 122.
καύσων, 154.
κειρία, 40.
κιβώτιον, 154.
κληρόνομος, 100.
κοιμῶμαι, 155.
κοίτων, 40.
κομβόω, 155.
κοράσιον, 154.
κρεββάτι, 154.
κρίνω, 125.
κρίσις, 100.

λαξευτός, 116.
λικμάω, 126.
λυχνία, 40.

ματαιότης, 113.
μεγαλειότης, 132.
μοιχαλίς, 116.
μονή, 154.
μωραίνω, 127.

νύμφη, 123.

ξενοδοχεῖον, 154.

ὀθόνιον, 40.
ὁλοκαύτωμα, 113.
ὁμιλέω, 155.
ὀνυχίζω, 40.
ὀπτασία, 154.
ὀχύρωμα, 123.

παιδεία, 101.
παιδεύω, 155.
παιδίον, 154.
παιδίσκη, 40.
παντοκράτωρ, 114.
παρεμβολή, 15.
πάροικος, 102.
πατάσσω, 127.
πατριάρχης, 114.
πειράζω, 106.

πιάζω, 155.
πίεσαι, 158.
πληροφορέω, 119.
πορεύομαι, 107.
προσευχή, 114.
προσήλυτος, 115.
πρόσκομμα, 154.
προσφάγιον, 154.
πρόσωπον, 123.

ῥαντισμός, 115.
ῥῆγμα, 154.
ῥῆμα, 124.
ῥύμη, 15.

σάρξ, 102.
σκληροκαρδία, 116.
σκύλλω, 82.
στήκω, 158.
στρῆνος, 41.
συζητέω, 155.

συνάγω, 128.
σωτήρ, 103.

τελωνεῖον, 154.
τρύβλιον, 41.
τρώγω, 82, 155.

ὑπάγω, 156.
ὑπουργός, 154.

φάγεσαι, 158.
φθάνω, 156.
φιμόω, 41.
φωλεά, 154.
φωτίζω, 107.

χάρτης, 42.
χορτάζειν, 82, 156.

ψηλαφάω, 156.

www.ingramcontent.com/pod-product-compliance
Lightning Source LLC
Chambersburg PA
CBHW050808160426
43192CB00010B/1684